A Better You Today for Tomorrow

A Better You Today for Tomorrow

You are special
God bless you
MLVassell.
10/31/15

Maizie Vassell

Strategic Book Publishing and Rights Co.

Strategic Book Publishing & Rights Co. LLC
USA | Singapore
www.sbpra.com

ISBN: 978-1-62516-307-3

Dedication

I dedicate this book to my father, Lenard Harriott, and Stepmom Jennifer Harriott, who have always believed in my potential and encouraged me in whatever I set out to do.

To my two beautiful daughters, Monique and Annakay, for being my source of inspiration. Their unconditional love and enthusiasm have been the driving forces behind my success. May they be blessed as they aim for excellence.

To my sisters, Angela, Joy, and Jillian; my brother-in-law Gordon; my nephews Jahvanie and Jason; and my one and only niece, Jade-Ashley. My sisters are there for me when I need them most.

To dear friends Doreen Lewis, Heather Brooks, Donna Collins, Donna Whorms, Omar Greene, Patrick Josephs, Solomon Peck, Eyon Reid, Reverend Douglas Gooden, and Pastor Dalton Stephens.

Last, but not least, to all my cousins, uncles, uncles-in-law, and aunts, especially my Aunt Serena who stood behind us after the death of my mother.

Acknowledgements

Thanks to God the father, who chose me to write this book. I never knew I had the potential until I followed the lead of His spirit. During the writing of this book, God taught me the importance of depending on Him for the tools I needed to accomplish the mission for which He had appointed me.

Thanks to all my relatives, friends, and well-wishers, who have motivated me by believing in the fact that I can do it.

Thanks to Sister Veronica and Pastor Baptiste, CEOs of the *Good News Chronicles*, for my first publication experience. May God continue to grant them wisdom and courage to accomplish the tasks for which they are called.

Table of Contents

Introduction

When God told Moses he would use him to lead the children of Israel out of bondage, Moses gave God a bunch of excuses. One of them was, "God, I am a man of slow speech." In other words, he was saying, "God I can't." God gave me the inspiration to write this book, but unlike Moses, I did not say I can't, but rather, "God if that is what you want then I know you will show me how." This is the end product, *A Better You Today for Tomorrow.*

The life we live today determines to a large extent the life we live tomorrow. Since we can only work in the now, we must make the best use of the now opportunities, rather than wait for those we are not privileged to receive until tomorrow.

God created us with the ability and potentials we need to enhance our lives. But we have to be able to see them and, with the help of God, use them the best way we know how to be the best we can be. Too many of us allow external forces to dictate who we are and who we should be. Only you can make that decision. You must know what you want to be and where you want to go in life. External forces have power only if you allow it.

A Better You Today for Tomorrow was written to help you understand who you are, the powers within you, and how to use them to achieve greater fulfillment and satisfaction.

The book is divided into four parts: Go for Your Dream; A Special You; You Are God's, and A Better You.

Part one shows you how to go for your dreams, starting with the smallest building block: the power of your thoughts.

In Part two you will understand how special you are by comprehending the unique talents and abilities only you can use to enhance the world of which you are a part. Without this understanding, you will never be able to see the value in you.

In Part three you will understand that you are God's and that this is vital. He is your creator, and, without an intimate relationship with Him, your life on earth will end without a sense of fulfillment. It is through God that you will understand the purpose for which you were created.

In Part four you will become a better you: the *you,* you set out to be. Evidence of your effort will be visual. You will be ready to join with God in bringing you to the level for which you were designed. You will feel a sense of relief when you hear, "Well done, thou good and faithful servant." The journey of yesterday ends with *A Better You Today for Tomorrow.*

Part One

Go for Your Dream

Chapter One

You Are Your Thoughts

Don't copy the behavior and customs of this world, but let God transform you into a new person by changing the way you think.

Romans 12:2, NLT

As a child growing up, I used to wonder *what makes a teacher look and behave differently from a doctor*. Certainly not the clothes they wear! What makes a Christian behave differently from a non-Christian? I would say "The blood of Jesus makes the difference." But as I grew to understand the power of the mind, I actually realized that it is the way people think that makes the difference. Proverbs 23:7 clearly states that "As a man thinketh in his heart so is he." In other words, you are your thoughts.

The mind is the most powerful component of a man's life. It is the breeding place of our thoughts. Our body, to a large extent, is constituted by our mind, which means, therefore, that without a mind we cease to exist.

Paul realized the importance of the mind when he said in Romans 12:2, "Don't try to copy the behavior and customs of the world but let God transform you into a new person by changing the way you think." That is why a born-again believer can say, "Things I use to do I will do them no more." This is as a result of a change in thoughts.

I was privileged to participate in a Gospel concert hosted by convicts and ex-convicts who became Christians while serving time at the Spanish Town District Prison in Spanish Town, Jamaica, West Indies.

I will never forget one young convict. Part of his left arm was missing and, with tears in his eyes, he testified, "I found myself begging for my life when I realized that very soon I would be executed. But then it struck me that I have no right to beg for my life when I have taken the lives of so many innocent people. I would see a man coming down the road and my thought said *kill him,* and I would shoot him down like a bird. I never valued the lives of people, so why should anyone value mine? Who am I to be begging for my life?"

Everybody in the audience was moved as he started to sing, "There is not one broken vessel that God can't mend."

In his book, *You'll See It When You Believe It*, Dr. Wayne W. Dyer writes, "Your actions come from your images." That is, the thoughts that have formed in your mind will influence the things you do. Christ performed a transformation in the minds of these convicts, thus, making them new individuals. In Christianity, it's the born-again experience.

If your life is built on negativity, it is the result of negative thoughts you are entertaining in your mind. Ralph Waldo Emerson said, "We are what we think about all day long." Thoughts are not just the things we do, but also the rest of who we are.

Your thoughts determine whether you live a successful life or one of failure. If you consistently think thoughts of prosperity, then you will be prosperous. If you want to be rich financially, emotionally, physically, and spiritually, you will have to think thoughts that will bring these results.

In his poem *Invictus,* William Ernest Henley wrote, "I am the master of my fate, I am the captain of my soul." You have the ability and the power to control your thoughts. Hence, you should refuse to blame where you are today on your loved ones, your family tree, your community, or your past failures.

Unwanted thoughts will come but that's what they are: unwanted. So tune them out and focus on that which is wholesome. Paul admonished us in Philippians 4:8 (TLB), "And now, dear brothers and sisters, one final thing. Fix your thoughts on what is true, and honorable, and right, and pure, and lovely, and admirable. Think about things that are excellent and worthy of praise."

Negative Thoughts Can Hinder Your Blessing

God created man as a perfect being, placed him in the Garden of Eden, and gave him dominion over the creation. But the greatest gift man was given was the ability to choose. God gave man instructions to not eat of the fruit of the tree of good and evil. He could have taken the appetite away from man, but he did not, as man was given the freedom to choose.

Satan, who knows that a negative thought hinders blessings, implants the thought in man that God's instruction is futile and that if he eats of the fruit, he shall not die but live. Hence, man succumbed to the temptation by partaking of the fruit of the garden. That was an easy way out. From that day, communication with God was never the same, and man's punishment was "by the sweet of thy brow thou shalt eat bread." (Genesis 3:19 NLT)

A negative thought is like the wall of Jericho: it is set to prevent you from enjoying the blessings on the other side. But just as the army went around the wall seven times as instructed, you also need to do all it takes to break down the wall of whatever is preventing you from walking the road to being a better person.

It is easy to allow negative thoughts to dominate you, as sometimes it takes less effort on your part. God says you have the ability to rise to supervisor level at your job, but you say *No*, because choosing no means you won't have to work so hard applying the skills necessary for the promotion.

I've heard it said many times that the path to hell is broad, while the path to heaven is narrow. It is man's tendency to choose the easy way out. But what a day it will be when the time of accountability draws nigh! You will be a loser if you do not rise to the challenge of maximizing your true potential. Just as the servants were called upon to give an account of the talents they were given, so too will you be called upon to give account of all that God has blessed you with.

God has made provisions for you to log on to good health and prosperity, but you may refuse to let go of negative thoughts and grab hold of the promises given by God. For instance, He promised you good health, but you felt a pain in your stomach and were told by your doctor that pancreatic cancer has taken over your body; that you only have ten more days to live. On hearing that, you gave up hope. You forgot that God's words supersede that of man; you forgot that there is nothing that God can't do; you forgot that man has limitations, but God is infinite.

I watched an interview between Patrick Swayze and Barbara Walters after Swayze had been diagnosed with pancreatic cancer. Some thought he would die five weeks after being diagnosed, but he refused to entertain negative thoughts that would rob him of the energy he needed to hold on to life. Instead, he stood firm in his belief that things would work out okay. Although today he is dead, his faith kept him going long after the diagnosis. Negative thoughts are so destructive that they sometimes produce physical ailments in our bodies.

My mom died from cervical cancer at the age of forty-five, and that time is still fresh in my mind after twenty-three years. I remember her pain and agony, and, as a result, I developed a great fear of cancer.

Sitting in the staffroom at Anchovy High School where I taught for a number of years, I overheard a colleague relating the story of her friend who had breast cancer. Prior to her friend's knowledge of the cancer, she felt an excruciating pain in the side of her breast towards her armpit. I remember my friend saying, "Oh, it was terrible."

Still thinking about the pain, I went home later in the evening and felt a pain in *my* left breast. My thought was, *Oh my God, don't tell me I am developing breast cancer*. Becoming really worried and frightened, I dialed the number of a nurse friend and said to her, "I feel a pain in my left breast, and I think I am developing breast cancer."

Her response was, "What makes you say that? Feeling pain in your breast does not necessarily mean that you have breast cancer. It could be a result of a number of reasons, but I would advise you to see the doctor. By the way, Maizie, it could be gastritis. Did you eat this morning?"

I replied, "To think about it, no. I was so busy today that I forgot to eat." Shortly after getting something to eat, the pain subsided. I never had breast cancer. Whatever is happening in your spiritual world will manifest itself in the physical.

Negative thoughts often prevent us from walking the road to success in our profession. I graduated from secondary school in 1984 with few CXC (Caribbean Examination Council) subjects. My principal was impressed with my performance. He wrote a letter to the principal of Church Teacher's College asking him to allow me a place in his institution, since it was too late to apply the usual way. But his effort failed, as all the places were already taken.

I went back to him and was given another letter, written by another teacher, whose daughter had a place at Bethlehem Teachers' College, but had decided to go to Church Teacher's College instead. I took the letter, but never went. I allowed negative thoughts to override my good sense of reasoning. I thought at that time that my parents could not afford to send me to college. By then, my other three sisters were in high school and it was financially difficult.

I came in contact with a student of Bethlehem Teachers' College who told me that the tuition was astronomical. Without consulting the college, I accepted that information, thinking that college was certainly out of my reach.

After moving from one job to another, I finally decided to pursue my dream of becoming a teacher. I applied to Bethlehem Teachers' College in 1991 and became a student there. I graduated a few years later. The most amazing thing was that my tuition at the end of college was not even half the cost the student had told me a few years before. The truth was the tuition was subsidized by the government.

If only I had understood the power of my thoughts, I would have taken up the challenge to seek information from the college, and I would have obtained my profession long before I actually did.

Don't listen to your negative thoughts. Don't allow them to dominate your life! "It is not by might nor by power, but by my spirit," says the Lord of Host.

I heard once that "Your success does not depend on your potential or ability, but on your faith."

Dr. Wayne Dyer further puts it, "The more negative your thoughts, the more likely you are to lack exclusively at the physical side of you, and to behave in such a way as to destroy your body as well. Every negative thought is an inhibitor to personal transformation. It keeps you clogged up just as cholesterol clogs up an artery. When you are filled with negativity, you are kept from achieving higher and more beautiful levels of happiness." So take control of your thoughts today and be a better you today for tomorrow.

Positive Thoughts Bring Positive Results

My sister, Joy, was accepted as a student of Bethlehem Teachers' College after I was. Motivated by my performance as a student of that same institution, she said to me, "Maizie, I will graduate with twice the amount of certificates and trophies that you graduated with." She certainly did! That was positive thinking and it resulted in positive rewards.

In his book, *Think and Grow Rich,* Napoleon Hill says, "Our brain becomes magnetized with dominating thoughts which we hold in our minds and by means which no man is familiar, these magnets attract us like forces, the people, the circumstances of life which harmonize with the nature of our dominating thoughts." Hence, if our thoughts are positive, we will see impossibilities become possible. Our mountains will diminish to mounds; our Red Seas will be parted to give us dry ground on which to walk; our bodies will be blessed with good health; we will start to reap financial blessings; our relationships will thrive in spite of the problems we encounter; and we will start to see the favor of God upon our lives.

A student at one of the schools where I taught came from a humble beginning. His mother would get up in the mornings and prepare his lunch to take to school. At one point, he was the only student to take lunch to school, but he never allowed pride to stand in his way and he wasn't intimidated by the negative vibrations around him. His positive attitude toward his work created an avenue for him to be promoted from the lowest class in grade seven to the highest in grade eight. He graduated as *Head Boy* with the highest achievement in the CXC examination. His positive thoughts produced positive results.

The psalmist admonished us in Psalms 84:11, "For the Lord God is a sun and shield; the Lord bestows favor and honor; no good thing does he withhold from those whose walk is blameless." (NIV) Get up and claim the blessings that God has in store for you and stop living your life in mediocrity.

God sent the partner he desired you to have, but you kept thinking that it can't be, as he or she is too good for you; that you can't walk in his or her category. How dare you think that! How dare you think that God will withhold what is good from you! Think positively and be blessed.

Maintaining positive thoughts takes willingness on your part. We walk by faith and not by sight. Your senses will dictate to you something differently from what faith demands of you. When faith says, "Step out on the water," you say, "No, faith, I can't! I can't swim, so I will surely drown." But faith says, "Put me to the test and see what I will do. I have made promises to you and I do not lie. I will never leave you alone. I will be by your side every step of the way. I will activate providence and give that which you have always dreamed of. Just watch me!"

Jesus said, "Do not worry about what you shall eat or drink or what you shall wear. These dominate the thoughts of unbelievers but your Heavenly Father knows your needs." To maintain positive thoughts when the economy is bad, or when there is no money in your pocket, takes willingness. But because God is faithful to his words, he never lies and cannot lie. You are going to be optimistic and say, "Though I don't know where my next meal is coming from, I will wait on the Lord; though I don't know where the money is coming from to pay my tuition, yet I will apply to college." Having willingness is to say like Esther, "If I perish, I perish."

I was told that, as a baby, I was so sick no one thought I would live. My parents told me they had gone to several doctors but the prognosis was never known. And in spite of their failed attempts to get me well, my parents never gave up. They continued to put their trust in God, their healer, and today I am alive and well. Positive thinking brings positive results.

The fact that you control your thoughts means that you can decide whether to be happy or not, whether to be depressed or not, whether to be successful or not. Do not allow the cares of life to press you down. Cast your burdens on the Lord and move with the flow. Many times we say, "Yes, Lord, here it is," but before we leave the burden, we take it up again with the weight pressing us down. An unknown poet puts it this way:

Let Go and Let God
As children bring their broken toys
with tears to us to mend,
I brought my broken dreams to God
Because he was my friend
But then, instead of leaving him

in peace to work alone,
I hang around and tried to help
with ways that were my own.
At last I snatched them back and cried,
"How can you be so slow?'
"My child," he said,
"What could I do?
You never did let go."

As a child growing up with no running water at home, I usually had to go to the public pipe to get water. The worst part was when I went to the nearest pipe and there was no water, I had to find another pipe as it made no sense to go home without water. Sometimes I had to walk almost half a mile to get water. I didn't want to make several trips to the pipe after having travelled so far, so I would carry a large bucket that held a lot of water. Though it was hard to carry, I preferred that to having to make several trips.

One day I remember carrying a five-gallon bucket and had problems lifting it to my head. I had to wait until I could get help to lift it. But no matter the thickness of the cushion that was between my head and the bucket, the weight was sometimes too much for me. I was so anxious to reach home. And what a relief after it was lifted from my head! I felt light and free again. That's exactly how it feels when you leave your burdens with the Lord.

Today, decide in your mind to be happy. Think happy thoughts; think thoughts that will put a smile on your face at all times. Doing this will confuse those who wish you failure in your endeavors; it will bring your enemies to their knees. Remember that "no weapon that is formed against you shall prosper."

Keep the remote control for your thoughts close at hand. When the negative channel tunes in, switch with urgency to the positive. This takes a conscious effort, but I can assure you that you will receive the most favorable result. The song says:

Don't let Satan see your fears,
Try to smile through your tears,
Hold your head up high and give the world a smile.
You must be faithful all the way,
It'll be worth it all someday
For your trials will be over in just a while.

Living above Negative Labels

The story is told of a florist who always got his messages mixed-up. One day, something terrible happened. He was told to send flowers to a newly married couple as well as to a local friend. But he got the cards all mixed-up! The newly married couple got the message, "Our deepest sympathy to both of you," and at the funeral, the local friend got the message, "Good luck in your new location." As a result, his business went under.

Negative labels are mixed-up messages! They relay information about you that is not true. And I don't care who it is coming from. It could be from your parents, your teacher, your psychologist, or the board of education. It doesn't matter. The only person who has the right to label you is your creator. You are his inventory. He knows more about you than you know about yourself. He knows you by name and number. He counted the number of hairs on your head. The inventor of the first motorcar knows more about its potential than the person who buys it and calls it his own.

In Jeremiah 29: 11-19 (NLB) God is saying to you, "I know what I am doing for you. I have it all planned—all plans to take care of you, not to abandon you, plans to take care of the future you hoped for. When you call on me, when you come and pray to me, I'll listen. When you come looking for me you will find me, yes when you get serious about finding me and want it more than anything else, I'll make sure you won't be disappointed. I'll turn things around for you." That's God's promise to you. So no matter what label you are given, you do not have to believe it, as it is not true.

In his book, *Live Your Dreams*, Les Brown tells the story of how he was labeled as "educable mentally retarded" in fifth grade, a label that rested heavily on his spirit. As a result of such a label, he put no effort into doing well. He settled for Fs, as no one expected better from someone who had such a label. But a special-education teacher, Mr. Washington, made all the difference in his life. One day in the class, Mr. Washington called him to the board to write something and Les's response was that he could not. When he was asked why not, he responded, "Because I am educable mentally retarded."

Mr. Washington got angry and told him that he never wanted to hear him say that again. He further intoned, "Someone's opinion of you does not have to become your reality." And that made all the difference in Les's life.

You too do not have to believe everything people say about you. It is up to you if you want to grab it and run with it, thinking that it must be the truth.

A friend told me how one of her high school teachers said, in the presence of other classmates, that she would never come to anything worthwhile in life. From that day on, she decided in her heart that she was going to prove that teacher wrong. She worked hard through high school and did well in her external examinations. As a result, she applied for and was accepted as a student in a teachers' college. From there, she pursued her first degree at a university. At the beginning of her final year, that very same teacher was there as a first-year student working on her first degree!

After her final exam as a third-year student, my friend went to greet the teacher and reminded her of the label she had given her years before. (No hard feelings.) The teacher told her she was sorry and encouraged her to continue to aim high.

I have often said to colleagues, "Be careful of the label you put on students, as life has a way of turning on you. Some of our students will leave school better than how *we* left and will take up positions in society that are higher than where *we* are right now. As a matter of fact, it should be our aim as teachers to see our students take their rightful places in society."

As parents, we also have to be careful about the labels we put on our children. As a result of negative labels, they can grow up with very poor self-esteem.

I had met a man who was raised in one of the southern states. He related how he grew up with abusive parents and, like Les, was given the label of educable mentally challenged, but, unlike Les who lived above his negative label, this man almost became lost in the frightening shadows of society—he had never learned how to live above such a label. Consequently, he stopped going to school before finishing fifth grade. Having no peace in his home, he took to the streets and became involved with the wrong group. He started taking drugs, became a part of a gang, and eventually found himself homeless. Many times he was shot at, but God spared his life. This man made several attempts to escape this kind of life, but it kept starring him in the face. In his mind, he probably was thinking that there was no better way out; that he was a good-for-nothing. His self-esteem was damaged. He had no love for himself, hence, dug deeper into drugs—his way of escaping the bitterness of a savaged reality.

But one day, in a state of despair, he said he acknowledged two choices put to him by God: life or death. He chose life, as he had never wanted to die. He was tired of running, of hiding, of being nobody. He was in his early forties when he decided to make a change in his life. Today he is celebrating his new life in Christ. When one comes in contact with Jesus, he or she is never the same. He came that we may have life and have it more abundantly. This man experienced a transformation. His thoughts were changed from a negative state to a positive one. He no longer thinks himself as nobody. He is now experiencing a life of hope, joy, and peace.

When the devil tries to convince you that you are nobody and do not deserve life, look him in the face and tell him that he is a liar. Say to him, "I am somebody, no matter what you think." When he tries to tell you that you will never make it, tell him, "'It is not by might, nor by power, but by my spirit,' says the Lord of Host." Tell him that it is not up to him what you become in life; it is up to you and God, who will give you the directions you need to live a fulfilled and purposeful life.

The fact is, you do not have to obtain a university degree in order to be worthwhile in life. You don't have to be like the Joneses in order to make it in life. Neither do you have to be born in a so-called rich environment to be who God created you to be. You are special. You are unique and can be anything you want to be in life as long as you take up the challenge to rise to the height of your potential and abilities. You have your own style of achievement with all the necessary tools in place for you to make the leap to success. Tell yourself that you can—and go for it.

Chapter Two

What You Say Is What You Get

For verily I say unto you that whosoever shall say unto this mountain be thou removed and be cast into the midst of the sea and shall not doubt in his heart that those things which he saith shall come to pass, he shall have whatsoever he saith.

Mark 11: 33

"I can't take it anymore."

"Life will never be better for me."

"I stopped trying. Everything I tried failed."

"I am fed up with life."

Do these words sound familiar to you? Sure they do. Perhaps, these are words you have been speaking all your life! No wonder you feel depressed and unfulfilled. You feel that life has nothing to offer you and that all is lost. Sickness takes over your body, your marriage is failing, your business is collapsing, and the dream you once had is buried, never to be resurrected. Absolutely nothing is working for you. But the good thing is that you are not at the end. You can break down the stronghold of oppression, poverty, hatred, and crime and speak prosperity, love, and peace in your life. Change your words today and watch supernatural things start to happen in your life. Your moment of reinvention is at hand. Speak the word and let it be.

The Power of What You Say

Thoughts, words, and deeds are identical in that what you think becomes what you say and do. The words you speak and the things you do are not independent of thoughts. Hence, whether your thoughts are negative or positive, you will speak or do things to reflect negativity or positivity. Many times in life we take for granted the words we speak without being conscious of the fact that what we say is what we get.

Jesus was on his way from Bethany and was hungry. He noticed a fig tree in full leaf and went over to see if he could get some figs to eat, but there were none, only leaves. Then he said to the fig tree, "May no one ever eat your fruit again!"

The next morning the disciples passed by the fig tree and noticed that it had withered from the roots up. Peter remembered and said to Jesus, "Look, rabbi, the fig tree you cursed has withered and died!"

Then Jesus said to his disciples, "For verily I say to you that whosoever shall say to this mountain be thou removed and be cast into the sea and shall not doubt in his heart that what he saith shall come to pass, he shall have whatsoever he saith."

My friend, whatever change you want to see in your life, you can have it simply by speaking it into existence. You do not have to go around blaming your present situation on your family background, your friends, your community, your broken marriage, or on a former teacher. You can, right now, change the course of your life by speaking exactly what you want to see happen. You may have been told many times that you will come to nothing worthwhile in life, but that's not true. That's a lie from the pit of hell, and you must not believe it.

Start telling yourself you can be anything you want to be in life; that you can achieve any goal you set out for yourself in spite of your present situation. What you say is what you get; the words you speak are powerful.

In his book *Believe in the God who Believes in You*, Robert H Schuller has this to say: "Words are incarnation of emotions. A word can either be a balm or a bomb." In other words, words can either make us or break us.

I remember when I was around fifteen years old and went into Mr. Allen's shop in the community where I grew up. You could get products there that you could never get anywhere else. Mrs. Allen was serving at the time. I ordered a tin of Vaseline, as I wanted it to create my own lipstick. (Don't ask me about it now. I will tell you later.) After handing the Vaseline to me, Mrs. Allen said, "Maizie, I think God spared your life for a special reason." She went on to tell me how sick I was as a child and that everyone thought I was going to die. That never left me. As a matter of fact, it helped to shape me into who I am today. The truth is, God is not finished with me yet. He is still in the process of molding me to be the perfect vessel he intended me to be. Proverbs 16:23 says, "From a wise mind comes wise speech; the words of the wise are persuasive."

Spoken words can enhance your whole outlook on life. They can help you see the impossibilities as possibilities; life rather than death; health rather than sickness; riches rather than poverty; love rather than hatred; and fulfilled dreams rather than unfulfilled ones.

There are many who have gone on before you who have never spoken their dreams into existence, so don't let this happen to you. Start speaking your dreams into reality. The Lord promised to supply all our needs according to his riches in glory, hence, instead of speaking scarcity in your life, start speaking prosperity. Likewise, instead of speaking ill-health, start speaking good health. Say, "I will not allow how I feel or what the doctor said have a negative influence on my faith in God; I am going to be healed. I will not worry that my children will never make it in life, for God promised to be with them all the way. He said 'Suffer the little children to come unto me and forbid them not for such is the kingdom of God.'"

You may have made wrong decisions in your life but, hey, who of us has not made such decisions? Stop fighting yourself and be the free agent God intended you to be. He wants you to speak with freedom, prosperity in your marriage, prosperity in your finances, and prosperity in your business. Rise up to the task and preserve your name by being all that God wants you to be.

Stay Right Where You Are and Speak Blessings in Your Life

Recognizing where you are right now is important if you are to speak blessings and more blessings into your life. You don't have to wait until you are in a foreign country, or wait until you have enough money. If you want to be blessed and receive all that God intends for you to have, you have to speak now. Tomorrow may be too late.

A very good friend of mine with the potential to be a journalist was encouraged to pursue the field, but she kept putting it off, waiting for the perfect opportunity. Thomas Edison wrote, "Opportunity is missed by most people, because it is dressed in overalls and looks like work." After over twenty years, the moment is still not perfect and she is right where she has always been. No movement. You see, that is the problem. If you do not learn to speak from where you are, you will never make a move. Opportunities will keep passing you in the same position and you'll be like a monument in the park.

There are a lot of people who put their lives on hold with the hope of moving after they have won the lotto. But what if you are among those who will never win? You will continue to sit and wait for nothing. Then suddenly, you realize how far time has gone. I have always said to people that it is appointed unto man once to die and death is an appointment that we all have to face. Therefore, let us see each day as an opportunity to fulfill the purpose for which we were created.

You can stay right where you are and make changes you want to see in your life by speaking them into existence with confidence and authority.

Napoleon Hill tells the story in his book, *Think and Grow Rich*, of Edwin C. Barnes, who wanted to be a business associate of Mr. Edison. He did not say that he wanted to work *for* Mr. Edison; instead, he said he wanted to work *with* Mr. Edison. Each time he told himself this, his desire became greater. He never knew Mr. Edison, but was determined to go to New Jersey to meet him. Though he never had enough fare, he boarded the train with enthusiasm to meet Mr. Edison. You see, he never waited until he had enough money. He started right where he was.

Barnes eventually reached New Jersey and, after presenting himself to Mr. Edison, told him that he had come so he could go into business with him. Mr. Edison was very surprised. He probably thought this man was mad. But something stood out to Mr. Edison: the determination on Barnes's face. And as a result, Barnes was given the opportunity to work for Mr. Edison. But this was not what he wanted. You see, he never lost sight of the fact that he wanted to be an associate of Mr. Edison.

Months went by and nothing happened, but Barnes never stopped saying to himself, "I came here to go into business with Edison, and I'll accomplish this end if it takes the remainder of my life." Eventually, he became partners with Mr. Edison and made millions of dollars.

You too can speak your dreams into reality. One day I said to my children, "Mummy is going to be rich." They laughed and asked, "How Mummy?" I remember saying to them that God had made a promise to me that he would bless me with silver and gold, houses, and lands. I may not know how, where, or when, but I know if God says so, then it shall come to pass. Although I am still waiting, I will continue to speak prosperity until it is evident in my life. Remember that "If you shall say to this mountain be though removed and be cast into the midst of the sea and shall not doubt in thine heart that whatsoever thou saith shall come to pass then it shall come to pass."

What words are you speaking today? The Lord asked you to come as you are. Stay right where you are and speak words of wisdom and power, words that will bring about a change in your direction, change from poverty to richness, from death to life. Tell yourself that you are going to be the wife or husband God wants you to be, the daughter or son He wants you to be, the dreamer He wants you to be.

You Too Can Speak Your Dreams into Reality

On my way home after visiting my sister at Hampton High School in Jamaica, I stopped at the front gate of Bethlehem Teachers' College and watched a group of students enjoying a game of netball, a game I love, but never learned to play. I stood there for about twenty minutes, and before I left I said to myself, *One day I will be a student here*.

I continued to tell myself that, and something started to happen—I started to talk like a teacher and act like a teacher. In my mind, I was a teacher. A gentleman asked me one day, "Are you a teacher?"

I answered, "No, but I'm hoping to be one soon."

He said, "I think you will be a good one." That has never left me.

After I got married, while working as a junior staff member at Appleton Estate, I decided that it was time to go for my dream. The path was certainly not an easy one, but that never stopped me. There were moments when I felt like giving up, but each time I told myself that I had come too far to turn back now.

Towards the end of my first year, I became pregnant with my first child. It wasn't an easy pregnancy, but I made up my mind to do well and I did. After giving birth to a beautiful little girl, I decided to spend a year with her, which I have never regretted.

Having to leave her to go back to college was painful, but I was determined to finish what I had started.

You too can speak your dreams into reality. All that you ever dreamed of becoming is already in the universe, but you have to be willing to speak it into life. Speaking it helps you become focused, which is important if you want to achieve anything in life.

Another friend, after finishing his first degree in real estate, was offered a teaching position in a well-known university in Jamaica. He refused, though the package was fairly good. That was not the dream he was speaking at the time. He dreamt of starting his own business in the United States of America. Today, if you should ask him if he regretted it at any time, he will tell you "no," because he successfully spoke his dream into reality and is doing well. Was it easy? I am sure he will again tell you "no."

From observation and experience, I have identified at least two things that happen when we speak our dreams:

1. Our words act as catalysts; they energize us and help us reach for that which we hope for. Then providence steps in to provide us with all the necessary resources needed for the dream to be accomplished.
2. We will be held accountable. Whether we speak to ourselves or to others, immobility will activate the guilt button, which, when applied in honesty, will allow us to become uncomfortable until mobility is restored.

Today, do not hesitate to speak blessings into your life. Don't wait for tomorrow. Don't think that you can't, because the truth is, you can. So practice and speak life into your dreams.

Chapter Three

Go for Your Dreams

Have I not commanded thee? Be strong and courageous, be not afraid, neither be thou dismayed, for the Lord thy God is with thee withersoever thou goest.

Joshua 1:9

In the final days of my grandfather's life, on Thursday nights the grandchildren sat at his feet, listening to him tell us Anancy and Duppy stories, which were part of the culture in which I was raised. Anancy and Duppy stories are folk tales, in which Anancy refers to the spider and Duppy to ghosts. After he finished, he would say to us, "Do not come back tomorrow though!" He was a Seventh Day worshipper, and his Sabbath starts on Friday evening.

One night Grandpa told us of the Duppy called Chip-Chip, who was afraid to walk at night unless he had company. Duppy was afraid? I thought that only humans were afraid! Nonetheless, we found the story quite hilarious. Grandpa loved when we enjoyed his stories. But little did he know the effect such a story had on me at night when I had to sleep alone. I would be up most of the night thinking that if I fell asleep, Chip-Chip would come after me or I might see him in my dreams. I don't think Chip-Chip was more afraid than I was. Whether I liked it or not, sleep consumed me.

Going for your dreams, however, is not about the nightmares that you sometimes experience when you sleep at night. I'm talking about the conscious dreams you experience when you are awake. I'm talking about the walk you sometimes take in your imagination; that desire you have to give positive contribution to your family and to society as a whole; that desire to be what God called you to do.

The power of the mind and its imagination are amazing. One can actually create what he or she wants to be or do in the mind. You can actually see what you want to be in the next five or ten years or even within a shorter time frame. The fact is, whatever you perceive in your mind, can actually become a reality. Isn't that great! But you may say, "I don't dream." That's not true. All of us are dreamers. We were made to be dreamers, though we do not all have the same dreams. Do you remember in primary school when you were asked to tell what you would like to be when you grew up? During my time, I can't remember anyone ever saying, "I want to be a criminal!" The most violent student would say, "I want to be a policeman," or "I want to be an air hostess," even when he or she had no idea what a policeman or air hostess was. We are all dreamers.

The problem we face, however, is that sometimes we are afraid to pursue our dreams due to a lack of self-confidence or because of fear, anger, guilt, and procrastination, to name a few. In Joshua 1:9 God offers you the consolation he gave to Joshua: "Have I not commanded thee? Be strong and of good courage, be not afraid neither be thou dismayed, for the Lord thy God is with thee withersoever thou goest." Hence, you need not be afraid. Dream big and go for it.

Discovering Your Purpose in Life

Have you ever been introduced to a new program that you didn't understand the relevance of until it was properly explained? I remember when I was first introduced to calculus in college. I could not understand it, because that I could not see the relevance of it in my everyday life. I presumptuously asked my tutor to tell me why I needed to learn this. After the possible applications were explained, I could see the purpose and, as a result, learning took place. So it is with life in general. You may ask, *What is my purpose in life? Why am I here? Why was I born?* I have asked myself these questions, too. Sometimes when I am alone in deep meditation I ask, *God, why did you spare my life when everyone thought I would die?* But each time I ask the question, I am assured that I am here for a purpose. You are, too. "Yes, I know that" you may say, "but what is the purpose? I don't have any special talent or ability. I didn't even perform well in school. I am now fifty years old and what have I achieved in life? Nothing!"

Earlier in this book, I mentioned that we were all created for a purpose, and I will continue to emphasize this fact, as it is very important for us to understand that God is not a time waster. When He took the lump of clay and molded us into His image, it wasn't because He had nothing else to do, but, rather, because He intended to create us with a sense of purpose. All of creation is as it is for a purpose. So, even though I am afraid of snakes and scorpions, they too were made for a purpose, even if they were meant to scare me to death!

Man is the most valued of God's creation. He took great care in creating you and me the way we are to bring Him glory. We were made with a wealth of potential that is hidden so deep within that it takes the power of the Holy Spirit to reveal it to us. With this comes the wisdom that He gave us to understand the revelation as to why we are here. It is the wisdom to understand that great desire within us that is making us so uncomfortable when we refuse to unfold it. Instead we reach for something that does not require much effort. We feel unfulfilled and uncomfortable because we are in the wrong place, at the wrong time, doing the wrong thing. In his book *Understanding Your Potential*, Myles Munroe writes, "There is no fulfillment in life without understanding the reason for being."

It doesn't matter whether you were classified as a mistake—as some parents allow their children to think—or that you were labeled a nobody, you were born for a purpose and, until you become aware of this purpose, you will never feel joy, happiness, contentment, peace of mind, and a motivation to be the best that you can ever be, no matter what it costs.

Your purpose in life gives you direction, which is constant. It never changes. It is the central theme of your life and on it hangs all your dreams. It is like a written lesson plan. In college, I was taught to write the general objective from which the specific objectives are derived. For instance, suppose the general objective is that the students will develop an understanding of sets, then the specific objectives should be aimed at allowing the students to understand the concept sets. Having the multiplication of fractions as one of the specific objectives would not help the students understand sets. At the end of the lesson, you would want to test the students to see if the objectives were achieved, hence, you would prepare your culminating activities. Likewise, if after achieving your goals, you do not feel inner peace and contentment, it could be an indication that you are heading in the wrong direction. You may have to stop right where you are and ask God for redirection, so that the purpose for which you were created can be fulfilled.

Have you ever heard anyone say that, after pursuing a career for a number of years, they realized they were not getting the satisfaction they should have been getting, until they actually followed their inner voice that had been seeking their attention all those years? If you ask God to reveal to you your purpose in life, He will. "Commit thy way unto the Lord and He will direct your path."

In seeking your purpose in life, it is also helpful to look on the qualities with which you are blessed. Are you kind, happy, joyful, loyal? What are some of the things you like to do? Do you like to encourage others to cook, or do you like to explore? After answering these questions, write a statement starting with

"I am—." For instance, "I am a cheerful giver." The fact is, however, if you are not connected to God, you will never know for sure the purpose for which you were created. Only the Holy Spirit can reveal this to you as, "No eye has seen, no ear has heard, no mind has conceived what God has prepared for those who love him—but God has revealed it to us by his spirit." (1 Cor. 2:9-10)

Reaching for Your Dreams

Person A and Person B were conversing on the phone.

Person A: Hi, girl. What're you doing?

Person B: Nothing, just hanging in there.

Person A: What are you doing with your life?

Person B: Nothing, just waiting for the right moment. They say nothing happens before its time.

Person A: I remember some time ago you said that you were contemplating college. Have you started yet?

Person B: No, as I said before, I am waiting for the right time. Don't forget! There's a time for everything under the sun.

Does this conversation sound familiar to you? Are you or anyone you know sitting around waiting for the right time to come? Well, many have sat around waiting for the right time and it never came. Do you know where they are today? Many of them are in the cemetery. They are buried with many bright ideas: poems that were never published; books that were not written; inventions that were never implemented; businesses that were not started. These smart minds did not have the courage to go after what they desired. Instead, they sat around waiting for time to tell them when to start. Now they will have to give an account of these ideas God gave them, which were intended to enhance His creation and bring Him glory. Luckily for you, you are still here and it is not too late. Start now, for now is the appointed time.

What is your dream? What is it that you've always wanted, but just did not have the courage to pursue? Or maybe you are afraid of what others will think of you?

My friend went to a graduation ceremony, and one of the graduates was a trained teacher, but she never felt that teaching was her purpose, so she joined the police force. Perhaps onlookers thought she was stupid, but she was not afraid of what people might say, and did it anyway.

Many people, when they are asked, "Why are you not doing what you love to do?" reply by making a list of the things they do not have. Not enough money, not beautiful, too old now—too many excuses. People who are always making excuses never reach very far in life. So stop focusing on the obstacles. The more you focus on them, the more they expand.

When I thought about writing this book, I didn't have a computer. I was doing a live-in job! But I made use of the library facilities and my spare time at work. I always made sure to bring to work books from the library, along with my writing materials. I never sat down and waited for a laptop to appear.

When you decide on the dream you want to pursue, do not allow anything to stop you. Write down the dream in details. Write down a time that you hope to bring it to fruition. The details should answer the questions: what, when, where, why, and how. Then commit it to the Lord so that He can direct your path. Do a survey of what you have already, including your qualities and resources. Continue to make a list of what you need, starting with first things first. Then start moving, a step at a time. It is said that "the journey of a thousand miles begin with one step."

For your dreams to be realized you must:

- ***Have a desire.*** This must be a burning desire. Make your dream an obsession. This desire will induce an enthusiasm. "Success is not the result of spontaneous combustion," says Reggie Leach, a retired Canadian Professional Ice Hockey right winger. "You must set yourself on fire." Visualize yourself accomplishing this dream and live it every day. This visualization brings with it power, and you will see God opening doors you never dreamed or imagined. The following Expedition by W.H. Murray says it all:

    > Until one is committed, there is hesitancy, the chance to draw back, ineffectiveness. Concerning all acts of initiative (and creation) there is one elemental truth, the ignorance of which kills countless ideas and splendid plans: the moment one definitely commits oneself, providence moves too. All sorts of things occur to help that otherwise never would have occurred. A whole stream of events issues from this decision, raising in one's favor all manner of unforeseen incidents, meetings, and material assistance, which no man could have dreamed would come his way.

- ***Make a commitment and be willing to stick with it.*** Be like Ester. When she decided to go to the King's chamber, it was against the law, but she had a cause she was committed to, so she decided, "If I perish, I perish." You have to make up your mind to take the risk, even if what you are about to do is not in everybody's favor. You will have to forsake all if need be. You may also need to turn an eight-hour workday into a twenty-four hour one, as my very good friend did. I thought at one point that he was crazy, but he was committed to the task at hand even when it never seemed logical to onlookers. Today, he is a successful businessman.

- ***Always do a progress check.*** See how you are doing. In teaching, we've got to do our progress check now and then by testing the students. The purpose is to test to see if our objectives were achieved. If not, we may have to reteach the topic and change the teaching strategies. Likewise with your dream, you will have to take a break and check how well you are doing. You may have to change some of the methods you were using to achieve the goal.
- ***Give God thanks in all things.*** Note that it is in all things. Not only when things are going well, as God may have just put a pause in to redirect you to a better path or to teach you a lesson or two to help bring your dream to reality. Remember God is able to divide the Red Sea to create dry paths for you to walk on; He can also make tunnels through your mountains. So give Him thanks in all things.

Overcoming Obstacles to Your Dream

Now that you are on the path of your dream, the devil will try persistently to get you discouraged and give you all the reasons why you will never make it. But I want you to look him straight in the eyes and tell him he is a liar and he belongs in the pit of hell. Don't be afraid of this monster as "Greater is he that is in you than he that is in the world." And "No weapon that is formed against you shall prosper." If God is for you, then tell me who can be against you. Let's take a look at some of the weapons the devil uses to get us to give up.

Fear is the most destructive of all human emotions. It acts as a barricade to prevent us from maximizing all the potentials with which we are blessed. It can hinder growth in all the areas of our lives. The fears most common in the path of our dreams are failure, past experiences, and success.

Maybe you are afraid to muster the courage to go after your dream because you think you may fail. But you will never know until you have tried. Failure is not always bad. We are cultured to believe that failure is the worst thing that can ever happen to us. But failure could be saying, "Hey! This is not the path you should not be taking; turn and go the other way." Failure is not an indication to stop. If at first you don't succeed, then try again. A former pastor used to say to us young people, "If you can't run, walk. And if you can't walk, mark time, but don't stop." You may be striving for perfection, but "Have no fear of perfection," says Salvador Dali, "you'll never reach it." Human beings are prone to mistakes.

My father, though it took him many years to understand that not all songs have the same rhythm, never gave up playing the guitar. He failed many times, and was criticized for playing the wrong notes, but he never gave up. He kept working at it and in 2008 was awarded for playing guitar in church for over forty years. So don't give up because you have failed. Use it as encouragement to do better the next time.

Fear of past experiences is another obstacle to our dreams. A friend of mine once told me that he has a phobia about marriage. Of course, he is divorced and had a terrible experience. You too may have had bad experiences pursuing your dreams, but your bad experiences do not guarantee future failures if the lessons taught were learned. Past experiences teach us wisdom. They teach us what to expect and how to deal with the unexpected. Losing your home, for example, because you were unable to pay the mortgages, does not mean that you can't own another home. What it does perhaps, is to teach you good budgeting skills and to make wise choices.

Another fear that you may encounter is the fear of success. Sound strange? Yes, I agree, but a lot of people are afraid that if they are successful, they may not be able to handle the responsibilities that come with it. For instance, suppose your dream is to start your own business. Of course this comes with a lot of responsibilities—meetings to attend, deadlines to meet, interviews, handling finances, and fame. You think it will be too much so you refuse to even give it a try. But God is saying to you, "Be not afraid for I am with you. I have not given you the spirit of fear but of a sound mind." Don't be like the servant who got the one talent and hid it because he was afraid to invest it. Do you remember what his master said to him? "Thou wicked and slothful servant . . ." Don't let this be your fate. When God gives you a dream, He intended for you to bring it to fruition. So don't be afraid.

In addition to fear, unworthiness is another obstacle that you may be faced with. You may say, "My dream is to be married and have children. But nobody wants me, as I am not attractive enough. I never went to college. I only have a high-school diploma. The men nowadays want highly educated women." But how dare you entertain these thoughts! Remember, what you say is what you get. How dare you think yourself unworthy of the dream that God gave you. It doesn't matter what kind of family or educational background you have, God can do for you more than you ever dreamed or imagined. If you only knew the blessings He has in store for you, you would stop wasting time on negative thoughts and start getting busy to receive those blessings.

Procrastination is like a veil over our eyes blocking our view of opportunities; hence, it becomes another obstacle in the path of our dreams. This was a problem I had encountered on the path of my dream, and I had to utilize all my courage to put it behind bars, like a man who committed a felony. You too may be going through this right now. You may want to take the first step, but keep putting it off for another time. This certainly is not the smart thing to do, as your opportunities will fail to expand and become less significant.

As a procrastinator, you have the tendency to put off things until the last minute; doing the urgent things and not the important ones. But though the thing may be urgent, it does not necessarily means that it is more important. In college, I would sometimes leave studying for the last minute, and then the information was crammed.

Do what you have to do now. Don't wait until tomorrow. If fear is your problem, feel the fear and do it anyway. Make your commitment and stick with it no matter what. Prioritize your goals and deal with them accordingly. I have friends who think that going to college for four years is not worth it, because by the time they are finished they will be too old. But what they do not realize is that the more they postpone college, the older they get. It is always better to start now. Later on they will look back and say "If only I had started—"

Impatience is another obstacle to your dream. How many times are we reminded that "Rome was not built in a day?" You may be tempted to give up, because you have been at this one thing for so long and nothing seems to be happening. How many times have you prayed and asked God for his direction, but thought that God was taking too long? So you got up and started to do things your way, then realized that you couldn't do it on your own. "They that wait upon the Lord shall renew their strength; they shall mount up with wings like eagles; they shall run and not be weary; they shall walk and not faint; teach me Lord how to wait."

There may be many barriers to your dream, but the final one is the failure to make decisions due to the sacrifices you may have to make. Jesus said in His words that for us to follow Him, we have to forsake our mother and father. Going after your dreams will require sacrifices. You may have to step out on your own, leaving your family and friends behind. Abraham had to pack all he had and move to a place he knew nothing about. He stepped out into the unknown. Your decision may not be popular, but if you feel that that is what you have to do, then do it. Do all that it takes to make things happen.

Persistence Pays

During my years from primary to secondary school, all the houses I was placed in came in last. I was never fortunate enough to celebrate victory at the end of a sports day. Too embarrassed, I would try to escape the ridicule of my friends from the other houses by going home as quickly as I could.

At Teachers' College, the same trend seemed to follow me. For the first two years, my house came in last. Then I said to myself, *Oh no! At the next sports day, this will not happen. I have to do something to ensure that my house is not placed last.*

So the following year, a few days before sports day, the athletes for the cross-country race were getting ready to run the race. I changed into my physical education outfit and told my roommates that I was going to run the cross-country. Of course they laughed, because they knew I was not an athlete. About twenty minutes before the race began, I went onto the field, ready for my take-off. The sports coordinator looked at me and asked, "What are you doing here?"

I responded, "I am going to run the cross-country." He laughed, too. To them I was not an athlete, but in my mind I was. I was determined to give my house at least one point.

The race started, and I thought I was doing pretty well until about a quarter of the journey when everybody started to overtake me. By then I was so tired, I felt I like giving up. But I said to myself, *Come on, Maizie girl, you have reached too far to turn back now. Remember, perseverance coupled with zeal can accomplish what zeal alone cannot do.* So I ran, then walked, then ran, then walked until I reached the final time keeper, Mr. Mills.

He said to me, "You ran the race in x minutes." I don't remember what x was, as that was not a concern. All I wanted was to finish the race to give my house a point.

I reached the college gate and had to run the entire field to complete the race. But when I heard, "Go, Maizie, Go," I forget the tiredness and ran with what little strength I had left. I completed the race and gave my house the point. That year my house placed first, and for the first time I experienced the joy of celebrating a victory after sports.

Persistency pays. At primary school I learned this gem:

When a task is once began
Never leave it till it's done
Be the labor great or small
Do it well or not at all.

Someone once said that the race is not for the swift, but for they who endure to the end. Be persistent in pursuing your goal or your dream. Keep it always in view. Never lose sight of it for one minute and you will achieve success.

Have you ever come in close contact with insurance agents? They are so persistent that no matter the number of times you refuse to buy the policy they offer, they never give up and most times they achieve their goal. That's the same approach you must have towards your dream.

Fight the urge to give up; recharge your operating battery; start the ignition; and accelerate in the direction towards your dream. Again, you may come to a stoplight, but stay focused, for you have not yet reached your destination. Keep your eyes on the road and watch for the amber moments when you need to accelerate. Be ready for when the light changes, as delay may cause an accident. Remember you are the DRIVER, so keep your feet on the pedal.

Chapter Four

You Can Do It

I can do all things through Christ which strengtheneth me.

Philippians 4:13

For many years I suffered from what I called the *ask somebody else syndrome*. Though I knew within myself that I had the ability to do whatever I was asked to do, I allowed fear to dictate what I did from what I didn't do. I refused to face the fear and did whatever I was asked to do. But I noticed that responding negatively always made me feel like a loser or an underachiever. I started repeating silently to myself, "I can do all things through Christ which strengtheneth me," but it was mere repetition as I doubted the power of that verse.

During my teenage years, *McGuiver* was my favorite television show. I hastened to do my chores so as not to miss it. Nothing was impossible For McGuiver. No matter the situation he was faced with, he would always find a way to get out of it. He would use whatever was available to him at that moment. Discarded items were put to use, and always with a success.

One particular day I came to realize that McGuiver must think to himself that nothing was impossible if you set your mind to it. So in the Bible I took to church I wrote, "Maizie, just as nothing is impossible with McGuiver, so it is with you. You can do all things through Christ. Believe it with all your heart." And that brought about a change in my life. I refused to let fear control my life. I started feeling the fear and did things anyway. I was reminded of that famous quote from President Franklin Delano Roosevelt that, "the only thing to fear is fear itself."

This experience has taught me the power of the mind and what faith in God and in me can do. My impossibilities have given way to possibilities; sorrows turned into joy; misfortune to opportunities. Romans 8:28 says, "For we know that all things work together for good to them that love the Lord and are called according to his purpose." This verse helped me to be who I am today.

Throughout life your power of choice is constantly in the *on* mode. The only time it is in the *off* mode is when you die. You are and will forever make choices in this life. During the *on* mode, thoughts are always processing. Every thought that flows through your mind has an opposing force that produces the exact opposite of the central thought being processed. So for every *I can* thought, there is an *I can't*. When the positive thought says, *You can do it*, the negative (opposing) thought says, *You can't do it*. Hence there is always an ongoing battle in your mind. The problem is the number of times you succumbed to the defeating thought and wear the label *I'm a loser*. It is hoped that this chapter, which is the core to your reaching for your dream, will change the *I am a loser* label to *I am a victor*!

The Power of I Can

Riding a bicycle was not one of my dreams until I went to work at Aquaculture Jamaica Ltd. I tried several times before and could never get the pedals to move forward. Every time I tried to pedal forward, the pedals would go backwards, and then I would be on the ground with either the bicycle beside me or on top of me. One day at work, my manager said to me, "We are going to buy a bicycle for you so that you can be mobile to and from the ponds."

I exclaimed, "But I can't ride, Mr. T!"

He said, "You will learn."

Collecting samples of water from various ponds was sometimes not possible, as occasionally no driver was available to take me around; hence, learning to ride the bicycle was a must. I remember the first time I decided to give it a try. I put my bottles in the carrier at the back of the bicycle. All eyes were on me. It was known that I could not ride, so everyone was curious to see what I would do. Afraid to go on the bicycle, I pushed it to the first two ponds. Now out of sight, I got on it, talking to it as though it could understand everything I was saying, and said, "I am going to ride you, though many times I've tried and failed. But watch me, this time I am going to get it right." I went out every day to practice, and eventually I rode it! I was thrown many times to the ground, but I never gave up, as I knew that I was going to ride with proficiency.

When you are in danger, adrenalin is the body's natural way of preparing you for fight or flight. Similarly, when the mind is in danger of stagnation, *I can* is the adrenalin that ignites the power circuit within you. It releases your potential energy and gives you a desire, enthusiasm, and motivation you have never experienced before. *I can*, when spoken, energizes the forces in the universe to come to your assistance. Paul knew this when he said, "Who can separate me from the love of God? Neither death nor life—" can separate him from the love of God, that has empowered him with the *I can* mentality. You too can be blessed with this empowerment if you would change your thoughts from *I can't* to *I can*.

Here is how it works: When your dream becomes a burning desire and you are sure this is what God wants you to do, the outer wall of impossibilities will break down to give you power, energy, and vitality. You'll rise with vengeance to pursue the task ahead of you, thus bringing that dream to reality. When you are faced with obstacles, such as a lack of finance, you will say to yourself, "though I do not have the money yet, I know I can—;

though I may not be as brilliant as other members of my family, I know that I can—; though the sickness may be taking hold of my body, I know that I can—"

The Master of I Can

Jesus felt the need to feed the multitude following him. There was a little boy who had five loaves and two fishes. Jesus took the food, blessed it, broke it, and fed over five thousand people. And after all were fed, the disciples collected twelve baskets full. Isn't that amazing? If you say *I can* with the little you have and commit it to God, He will bless you in ways that are hard for the human mind to comprehend. Your dream will no longer be a dream but a reality.

I remember needing a belt for an outfit I wanted to wear to a function. I thought the one I had was inappropriate, so I mentioned to my mother that I would borrow one from my aunt. Mom's response was, "No you will not. Use what you have." That statement remained with me throughout life. You have to learn to use the little you have to do what God wants you to do, as that *little* is much in accomplishing the dream you are seeking to pursue.

The man sitting at the pool at Bethsaida wanted to be healed of his leprosy, but he could not get into the troubled water due to his inability to move by himself. So, he sat there waiting for somebody to put him in. When Jesus came, the man never hesitated to seek his help. Jesus then said to him, "Rise up, take up thy bed, and walk." The point is, though he had a disability, the leper did not give up hope that he would be healed. He maintained an *I can* attitude until opportunity presented itself. You too need to maintain that kind of attitude. Keep focusing on your dream. Keep telling yourself that you can, even when time moves into eternity.

It must have been an embarrassing situation for the couple who was getting married and their wine ran out. But fortunately for them, Jesus was there. He instructed them to fill some buckets with water, which they did and, miraculously, the water was turned into wine and, indeed, was a better wine than the previous one. When God gives you the desire to pursue your dream, stop telling yourself that you can't, because the fact is that you can. God has the power to turn your water into wine by using the raw material of an idea and making it into the finished product that will fascinate observers, even those who thought that your idea made no sense. You must believe that you can.

Saying or believing the phrase *I can't* has a way of putting a veil of darkness over our mind's eye, blinding us from the beauty within us. But *I can* has the power to unveil that darkness. The veil comes in varying forms. Sometimes it's the color of our skin, our family background, fear, lack of proper education, old age, youthfulness, only to name a few. But like President Obama, you need to take the veil from your eyes and rise to the challenge ahead in spite of the obstacles. Empower your mind with *I can* and the whole universe will celebrate your victory. Go ahead. Don't stop, for yes YOU CAN!

A former employer of mine suffered from a stroke which caused temporary paralysis to his left side. He had a long series of therapy and was actually told by one of the therapists that he would not be able to climb stairs again. But he knew that he could and reminded himself every day that it was possible if he put his mind to it and worked on it consistently. I often heard his wife saying to him, "Yes you can." As a result, a therapist was hired to come to the house at least twice per week and together they worked on climbing the steps at the front of the house. Today my former boss is climbing steps without assistance. As a matter of fact, the ramp at the back of the house is obsolete! In his book *Understanding Your Potentials*, Myles Munro says, "Everything is possible if in addition to the beauty within you, you will abandon yourself to an idea enough that you are willing to lose your life for it."

Your creative power can be released through the power of *I can*. It must have been a delight for the blind man when Jesus restored his sight. He probably started to do things he had never done before; things that he thought he wouldn't be able to do. It will be the same with you when you allow the power of *I can* to instigate creative actions that you never thought were possible.

I can will restore your life once again; a life that was buried in the rags of chronic depression; a life that stole the joy you once experienced; a life that dictates to you failure and defeat. *I can* has the power to raise you back to life just as Jesus raised the dead back to life. You will be empowered to rise to the challenge of living life to the fullest. It's been said that some people are dead at age twenty-five but were not buried until they were seventy-five. Give God thanks that you are not in that category! You may be dead, but not yet buried, which means there is a one hundred percent chance that you can be raised from the dead. Therefore, as of today, stand on your feet and say sincerely from your heart that

> I will arise to the challenges presented me
> Casting off feelings of inferiority and self-pity
> Acknowledging the purpose for which I was created
> Never to return from whence I came.

Be a Member of the 'I Can *Club*'

The *I Can Club* is a mind club and accepts members of all ages from all strata of society. Our CEO, Jesus Christ, the great I am, believes that you can overcome any barrier that serves to hinder you from maximizing your potential and giving life to your dreams. One of the benefits of joining this club is that it comes to you right where you are. It will meet you at your point of need. Hence, you do not have to bend yourself out of shape to attend meetings. You must however read all the details of this club before deciding to become a member.

Name of Club: I Can

Mission Statement: Club I Can is aimed at allowing members to maximize their potential, to develop self-empowerment, and to achieve that which once was thought impossible. The club will design programs and activities that aim to eliminate negative perceptions of self and allow each member to recognize the purpose for which he/she was created.

Motto: I can do all things through Christ which gives me strength.

Theme Song: I'll rise again, Ain't no power on earth, Can keep me down; I'll rise again Death can't keep me in the ground.

Requirement for Club: Members must have a burning desire to succeed in all their endeavors.

Rules and Regulations:

1. You must give a clear description of the dream you are hoping to pursue. Never use the word *can't*. It is an abomination to the club, a deprivation of your dream, and will earn instant termination of membership.
2. For every day until the goal is achieved, you must say at least twenty times to yourself, *I can do it.* Failure to comply will earn you two demerit points. A total of six such points will result in termination of membership.
3. Participation is a must. You can't be a member of club I Can if you do not participate. Hence failure to do so will result in membership termination.

(The goals and methods listed on your membership form will be your activities.)

CLUB I CAN Membership Form

(Kindly fill out all requirements on this form)

Name ....

Date of Birth ....

Address ....

Telephone Numbers

(home)…………….........(cell)……………...............................

Dream:...

Expected Time Of Achievement:

Goals listed in order of priority:

Description of goal……………Time…………Method...........

1. ....
2. ....
3. ....
4. ....
5. ....
6. ....
7. ....

(Achievement of each goal will earn you the YES I CAN medal)

Progress Report:..

....

Read the following carefully before signing:

I,…………., promise to obey all the rules and regulation of CLUB I CAN.

Date……............… signed……………………

- Club I Can has been around since the beginning of time. Adam and Eve were members of this club, but their membership was terminated because they were unable to abide by the rules and regulation. They were instructed not to use the words *I Can't*, but allowed the devil, who was also a member at one point, to influence them into believing that they did not have the potential to resist eating the forbidden fruit of the garden.

- Club I Can demands commitment. Hence, a lot of members have been expelled. Broad is the way that leads to destruction.
- It is hoped, therefore, that you will remain faithful as a member and that you will follow the footsteps of members who have earned their medals. They can be found in all strata of society. Some have served their full time here on earth and have left us a legacy to be enjoyed and protected. The question is, however, what do you want to be remembered for when you are gone? Use the power of *I Can* and be all that you can ever be. Your marriage will be restored; new sparks of enthusiasm will burst into flame; dreams once buried will be resurrected; the impossibilities will become possibilities. Rise up and be on the move with *I Can*.

Chapter Five

Opportunity Comes But Once

Behold, now is the accepted time; behold now is the day of salvation.

2 Corinthians 6:2

One of the most distressing statements I have ever heard is, "Life could have been better for me if only I had the opportunity like some people." But little did you know that many times opportunities came knocking at your door and longed to be acknowledged and welcomed, hoped to be wrapped in warm clothes, and be cuddled in loving, warm, enthusiastic arms. But, oh no! You were too lazy to go and see what was at the door. So opportunity, who did not want to die in the cold, went to another door. It is said that opportunity is never lost; someone will take the one you miss. When you are unwilling to give room to opportunity, somebody else will. The Jamaican proverb says, "Wha tan too lang serve neda man" or "What stays too long, serves another man."

Many times, our opportunities are missed because of our misplaced priorities. We are given the opportunity to get a good education, but we miss it by wasting our time thinking that there is always tomorrow, but oftentimes, it is too late. Now is the accepted time, now is the day of salvation.

I got a call from one of my daughters that a very good friend of mine was sick. I promised to call him, but kept putting it off another day. Every day I would say tomorrow, until about a week later, I got a call that my friend was dead. I was devastated. If only I had made use of the now opportunity and let my friend know how much I appreciated him.

On August 17, 1988, before I left for work, my mother, who was suffering from a terminal illness, got up and sat in a chair. I hugged her and told her good-bye, not knowing it would be the last time I would see her alive. If only I had known, I would have hugged her longer, kissed her, and told her how much I appreciated her. I missed this opportunity. As a result, I try to make use of all the opportunities I get to tell my children how beautiful they are, how much I love them, and that they are God's wonderful gift to us. It is important for us to live in the now to secure our future.

Opportunity is presented to us every day at every moment. Every difficulty that we face can be used as an opportunity. Romans 8: 28, which is my favorite Bible verse says, "For we know that all things work together for good to them that love the Lord and are called according to his purpose." Everything that happens in your life, whether good or bad, happens for a reason. Every person that you meet from day-to-day brings you an opportunity, even if it means just a smile. Maybe at that moment someone really needed another person to remind him or her that life is not all that bad.

In every negative there is a positive. From every experience, there is a lesson to be learned. Sometimes you may be wondering why things are not going the way you wish them to be, but you have to listen attentively to what God is saying, as He may just be telling you something or leading you in the direction He wants you to go.

A dear friend said to me once, "I am tired of praying and not getting an answer to my prayer. Isn't God listening to me?"

I said to her, "Yes, God hears and he listens to all our prayers, but the problem is we are not listening to what He is saying to us, because sometimes the answer is not what we want it to be."

Opportunity Comes to Those Who Look for It

God has blessed you with a dream, and He expects you to bring it to fruition. You have committed your goals to Him and have asked Him for his guidance in making this dream a reality. Now you must be on the alert and look for the opportunities that He will set on your path. It is important to note that when God asks you to do something, many times He gives you no details.

When God told Abraham to take his possessions and go to a land He would show to him, he never gave much detail, but Abraham followed anyway. When Isaac was promised to Abraham, God never told him when or how it would happen. When Peter saw Jesus walking on the water, and said, "Master, if it is you, bid me come unto thee." The only instruction Jesus gave was "Come."

Hence, when God gives you a dream, He expects you to take the first step into making it a reality, and He will furnish you with opportunities, which you will not see unless you are on the alert. 1 Cor. 16:13 says, "Watch, stand fast in the faith, be brave, be strong."

After my first job in the United States, I was at home for four months not working. It was a tough period for me, and every day I would take up my pen and paper and write about my experience. Sometimes it was in the form of a letter to God asking Him why? Sometimes it was in the form of a poem. One day as I was reading through all that I had written, I realized that I had a knack for writing that I never knew I had.

That period ended when I got a job as a caregiver. I was happy for the job, but very often I would ask myself, *what am I doing here with a first degree in education?* Again I started to write, and in so doing, my faith in God and what He was doing in my life illuminated. I started to look for opportunities and made use of them when they presented themselves, and that was when I started writing this book. Whatever experience God allowed me was intended to make me a better me for tomorrow.

Jesus said in Matthew 7:7, "Ask and it shall be given you; seek and ye shall find; knock and the door shall be opened unto thee." You will find opportunity when you ask for it; when you seek for it; when you knock for it. Hence, do not sit and wait for it, as it may never come. You will have to get out of your comfort zone and go look for it.

It was the year 2001 at the conception of the Bullock Heights Youth Club in Jamaica when the executives met and planned a dinner and gospel concert. We all agreed to invite a well-known gospel artist to be our guest. Unfortunately, the price was too high, so we had to think of an alternative.

After giving it much thought, I remember saying to myself, *I can sing and there are other members in the community who can sing*. Consequently, I went seeking. First I went to the Baptist Church and recruited two singers; then at the United Church, I got one; the Deliverance Center, I got one; and finally, from the Apostolic Church, I got one. We met, auditioned, started practicing, and called ourselves The Dynamic Gospel Singers. The concert was a success.

About a week after, we were invited to perform at another concert. Again our performance was great and a few weeks after that we were invited to be the guest artists at a concert in St. Ann, which was hosted by convicts and ex-convicts from the Spanish Town District Prison. From there almost every weekend, we were performing.

Still seeking opportunities, I was at a luncheon for teachers at Anchovy High School when we were entertained by a third-year student. He was an excellent singer, and I thought that he would be an asset to the Dynamic Gospel singers. Without hesitation, I asked him if he would care to be a part of our gospel group. His mother was contacted and he became a member of the group. That same year we were invited to participate in the biggest gospel show then, *Genesis*.

When you learn to go after what you want—to ask, seek, and knock—the opportunities will be presented to you. If you keep sitting down and expecting things to come your way, they may never come. You have to take an active part or you may be waiting for a long time.

If you want to lose fifty pounds, you will have to start your exercise program or whatever method you wish to use. Sitting down won't make it happen. If you want to write a book, start writing and opportunities will open to you. "When I look back into my life," said William Hale, "and call to mind what I might have had simply for taking and did not take, my heart is likely to break." So start looking for opportunities, as they come to those who look for them.

Make Use of the Opportunities, Even If They Wear Overalls

As I wrote this topic, the thought came to mind, *Never judge a book by its cover*. "Opportunity is missed by most people," said Thomas Edison, "because it is dressed in overalls and looks like work." I have had friends who have great business plans but refuse to make use of the opportunities, because they think it is too much work. Many students failed because the opportunity of a good education requires hard work. But success comes to those who are work-conscious. It is said that

> The heights by great men reached and kept,
> Were not attained by sudden flight,
> But they while their companions slept,
> Were toiling upward through the night.
> *Henry Wadsworth Longfellow*

Jesus highlighted opportunities wearing overalls when he told the parable in Matthew 25:41-46,

> Then shall he say unto them on the left hand, Depart from me, ye cursed into everlasting fire, prepared for the

> devil and his angels. For I was an hungered and he gave me no meat: I was thirsty and ye gave me no drink: I was a stranger, and ye took me not in; naked, and ye clothed me not; sick and in prison and ye visited me not. Then shall they also answer him, saying, Lord, when saw thee an hungered, or athirst, or a stranger, or naked, or sick or in prison and did not minister unto thee? Then shall ye answer them saying, Verily, I say unto you, inasmuch as ye did it not to one of the least of these, ye did not to me.

You miss your opportunities because they wear overalls, which most times act as a disguise. You won't truly know the value of the opportunity until you get up and take it as it is given.

Back in secondary school, I chose business education as my main course of study. I had the opportunity to do science, but paid little or no attention to it. I remember getting up in science class. I was feeling frustrated after having to leave typing class prematurely, and said to my teacher, "Sir, I don't like your class. I find it very boring."

Without evidence of anger, he responded, "Maizie, you better make use of this opportunity because you never know what the future holds." And he was right. In September 1991, when I started Teachers' College, I wanted to major in mathematics and science but my application was turned down due to my low science grade. As a result, I had to do primary education. Not that I regretted it, but if I had had a better science grade, I would have done what I wanted to do.

A man clothed in overalls indicates work. A surgeon going into the operating theatre puts on his overalls to protect his clothing; the mechanic will do likewise. You may not see the opportunity unless you are able to identify it in its overalls. Maltbie Babcock, a noted American clergyman says, "Opportunities do not come with their values stamped before them."

Giving life to your dreams requires you to get up and seek and that means work. I do not know a successful person who achieved success with folded arms. If his arms are folded, it is due to deep thoughts as to how he can achieve a particular goal, but they will not be folded for long. I will always make reference to a good friend of mine whose work day consists of thirty-six hours!

One common thing with opportunities in overalls is that they pave the way for greater opportunities. Wesley Autrey did not know he would be given the title *subway hero* and the opportunities that came with it, when he acted quickly to save an epileptic patient from being crushed by an oncoming train. He was interviewed by the CBS *Early Show*; he appeared on *Late Night with David Letterman*; he received a request to appear on the *Charlie Rose Show* and the *Ellen DeGeneres Show*; Donald Trump gave him ten thousand dollars; his two children were promised future scholarships, and he received a host of other opportunities.

At the workplace, you may aspire for the position of CEO, so make use of the opportunities presented you. Work hard at what you do. We are instructed in Colossians 3:17, "And whatsoever ye do in word or deed, do all in the name of our Lord Jesus Christ, giving thanks to God and the father by him." If we do, these doors of opportunities will be opened to us.

Be Ready for Opportunities When They Come Knocking at Your Door

If only I knew then, I would— Does it sound familiar? But hey! It is too late! Remember, friend, opportunity comes but once, so you must be ready to take hold of it when it comes.

A friend of mine who had always wanted to work on the Grand Cayman missed the opportunity because of unpreparedness. His neighbor had the opportunity to recruit some workers for a special work program on the Grand Cayman. My friend wanted to go into the program, but could not, as he had never had a passport and they could not wait until he got one. As a result, he was not recruited.

If you have a dream, do not sit down and wait for the appointed time. Start working on what you can now. Be ready for the opportunity train which will take you on an achievement ride. Do not allow the obstacles we have discussed in a previous chapter to prevent you from reaching for what you want.

It took Noah a long while to prepare the ark God instructed him to build. He was five hundred years old when he started and he entered the ark when he was six hundred years old. During that period, he warned the people to change their lifestyles and be saved from the flood that would destroy the earth. But instead, they mocked and jeered him. It started to rain and as the water started to rise, the people got scared, and wanted to be saved in the ark, but it was too late. The opportunity was missed.

Though faith will be discussed in the next chapter, I have to mention that many times we ask God for something and when it comes, we are not ready. If you are expecting rain you will walk with an umbrella. You have asked God to provide you with a husband and when he comes you are not ready. Many men and women today are not married as a result of unpreparedness for marriage.

If you find yourself in a situation that you do not like, ask yourself, "Why am I here?" Examine all the possible reasons and ask God for his assistance in finding the right reason for your being where you are. He might have placed you there to prepare you for what he has in store for you. When you are ready, he will pour out his blessings upon you which even you may not fully comprehend.

Chapter Six

Faith: A Prerequisite to Your Dream

Faith is having the confidence that you will receive that which you have asked for.

Hebrew 11:1

Therefore I say unto you, What things soever ye desire, when ye pray, believe that ye receive them, and ye shall have them.

(Mark 11:24)

I must have been about nine years old when my mother lifted her eyes to the sky and said, "Lord, give me faith."

My response to her was, "But, Mama, faith will give you the same problem!" She was hysterical when she realized I was referring to my cousin, Faith.

Many times when we are faced with problems we pray, "Lord, please give me the faith and courage to go through this." But here we are asking God for something that He has already given us! It is stated that, "To everyman was given a measure of faith." There was no partiality in the distribution of faith. Everyman was given his correct measurement. But though I may have been given a little bit more than you, you can use your little to remove mountains. "For if your faith is like a mustard seed you can say to this mountain be thou removed and be cast into the sea and it shall be done." As a result, any God-given dream can be accomplished by any man. In other words, no matter where you are in society, no matter your educational background, no matter your ethnicity, no matter the negative label you have worn throughout life, you can have that which you set out to achieve using the little faith you were given.

Hebrews 11:1 says, "Faith is having the confidence that you will receive that which you have asked for." The key is that you must have the confidence. You must believe. Once you start to waver, you will not receive that which you have asked for. "For a double-minded man is unstable in all his ways." No wonder you procrastinate! You must believe. Mark 11: 24 says, "Therefore I say unto you, what things soever ye desire, when ye pray believe that ye have received them and ye shall have them."

"Without faith it is impossible to please God because they that come to Him must believe He is the rewarder of those that diligently seek Him." (Heb 11:6) You cannot fulfill your dream without faith. It is a prerequisite.

"Even so faith, if it hath not works, is dead, being alone." (Jam 2:17) This verse is sometimes misinterpreted. Some people would argue that it makes no sense to have faith in something that you know will not work. But that's the catch for if you don't believe that it will work, it will never work. You have to believe. For instance, you want to go to college, but have not seen the first cent. How can you be thinking of starting college if there is no money? But if you have faith, you will believe that God will provide the money for college even when there is no evidence of such. Hence, instead of sitting doing nothing, you seek to apply to the college that you desire to go. It will surprise you where the money comes from. God is the God of the universe and he knows how to provide your needs. So even when the path gets very dark and you feel like giving up, don't give up. Put faith to the test.

When I first thought of writing this book, I knew that it was a God-given dream and though I may not be the best English scholar, I believed without a doubt that I could do it. Hence, I started to write. The more I write and move to make this dream a reality, the more God shows me that I can do it.

Faith does not depend on our perception. You do not have to actually see, hear, smell, taste, or feel it to know that bringing your dream to fruition is possible. Once you believe it, you will receive it. As a matter of fact, if you were able to see it, then there would be no need for faith.

Your dream may be to start your own school. The economy is in recession, and you have no money in your pocket, but if you believe that you can achieve your goal in spite of what is happening around you, then you will be surprised at what you can accomplish.

A former pastor of mine told the story of a man who asked God for a specific item and God sent the man to my pastor's house. Not knowing that the man had asked for this particular item, my pastor handed it to him out of sheer generosity. The man could not believe that God answered his prayer in such a quick and unique way. He lifted the gift, then turned his eyes towards heaven, and said, "God, why are you so tricky?"

Another man had nothing to eat, but prayed sincerely for God to provide him something to cook. Evening came and still there was no food. But because he knew that God would not let him down, he lit the stove and put on it a pot of water. A few minutes later, he heard a knock on his door. He opened it and was greeted by a neighbor who handed him a bag of food provisions! He lifted his eyes and gave thanks to God. That's how God works! Once you trust him to fulfill his promises in your life, he will not let you down. Even when the path is dark and the mountains seem too steep to climb, he will come through for you. Just simply put faith to the test.

The Five Essentials of Faith

1. ***The FOUNDATION must be solid***

   As children in Sunday school, we usually sang: *The wise man built his house upon the rock, The wise man built his house upon the rock, The wise man built his house upon the rock And the rain came tumbling down. The rain came down and the house stood firm . . .*

   The strength of your faith's foundation determines to a large extent the outcome of that which is hoped for. Your faith is like building a house. If the foundation is not strong, it will come tumbling down and destroy all that you have set out to achieve. Sometimes this is the reason for our broken dreams. A foundation built on the word of God will stand the test of time when the billows roll and the waves come dashing to and fro. No matter the obstacles that are set before you, your faith will remain unshakable. These obstacles will be seen as challenges instead of stumbling blocks. You will not be defeated but will be victorious. Such faith will remove mountains.
2. ***Your ATTITUDE must be positive***

   A positive attitude and faith are working partners. They are always seen together. One cannot function without the other. You cannot exercise faith when your attitude is negative; as a matter of fact, these two are enemies. They are always in opposition. And just as production goes down if the working force is not together, so it is with faith and negative attitude. You will achieve nothing. You may say, "Yes I have faith but—" You know, if the clause after the *but* is negative, that the statement is not a faith statement. In a faith statement, the clause after the *but* must be positive. You can't say, "Yes, I know I can cross the river but there is no bridge." Such statement is destructive to your faith. Your faith statement should instead be, "Yes, there is a river but I will cross over." Faith looks beyond impossibilities. Faith makes the impossible, possible. Faith sees a bridge even before it is constructed. Faith, with the right attitude, can change and accomplish what seemed impossible.

3. ***Your INTEREST is its energy***

   You can't exercise faith in something you have no interest in. Enthusiasm is a key element to your achievement, hence, there is no way you can perform a task if you have no interest in it. You will achieve nothing. Would you invest in something you have no interest in? Absolutely not. For faith to be invested you must have interest; you must be enthusiastic; you must be joyful; you must be creative; you must be on the alert. Know when to be in high gear and when to switch to low gear. No interest will produce a don't-care attitude, which is poisonous to your dream. Interest will motivate you to put out all you can: your time, money, and effort in achieving your goal. It will further motivate you to get all the necessary information on the dream you are hoping to bring to reality.

4. ***Your TRUST is the key***

   I tried to rotate faith to see if there was any angle where it could be exercised without trust, and I could not find any. You can't have faith in God if you do not trust him; you cannot have faith in your children if you do not trust them; if there is no trust in your partner, then the faith that your relationship will survive is useless. Likewise, you can't have faith in your dreams if you do not trust that they will come to pass. Faith is trust spelt another way: F (T), A (R),

I (U), T (S), and H (T). You can't have one without the other. In this case they are the same. They have the same characteristics, same potential, and same outcome. Trust is essential for faith to work.

5. ***Your HUMILITY is the key***

You may ask why humility is necessary to exercise faith. In all the miracles recorded in the Bible, all the recipients were in a humble state. I can recall the Roman officer who requested his servant be healed, but didn't think himself worthy of Jesus coming to his house. As a matter of fact, he didn't feel worthy to meet Jesus. So he said, "Lord, don't trouble yourself by coming to my home, for I am not worthy of such an honor . . ." (Luk 7:1-10) The woman with the issue of blood pushed her way to the Savior thinking only of touching the hem of his garment. Faith does not work with an arrogant and proud spirit. For your dream to be fulfilled, you have to learn how to be humble. You can't pray for your family to be reunited if you are going to allow pride to prevent you from saying *I'm sorry* when you know you are in the wrong. You may not receive the finances necessary to pay your tuition if you are not willing to let go of name-brand products or if you are not willing to do a mediocre job!

Think of all the people you know who are achievers. At some point in their lives, they have had to forget themselves in order to reach where they wanted to go. Your business may be on the downside but because of your pride, you refuse to seek help. The Bible says, "They that exalted themselves shall be a base, but they that humbleth themselves shall be exalted." Faith requires humility for it to work. You will have to start at the lowest rung of the ladder before you can reach the top.

The Five Natures of Faith

1. ***Faith helps you to be FOCUSED***

   It is the tendency for human beings to become distracted. We move around like gyroscopes, spinning around and ending nowhere. James 1:6-8 says, "But let him ask in faith, nothing wavering. For he that wavereth is like a wave of the sea driven with the wind and tossed. For let not that man think that he shall receive anything of the Lord. For a double-minded man is unstable in all his ways."

   For faith to show its true nature in your life, you have to remain focused. Though situations around you may threaten your faith and make you think that you are wasting time, that what you longed for will never come through, hold on and never let go. Develop confidence in the fact that whatever you hoped for will come to pass.

   When you are focused, you will keep your mind on that which you hoped for, your energy will be increased, and you will be raised to a higher ground from where you are presently standing.

2. ***Faith AMPLIFIES your dreams to give you a view of the bigger picture***

   It allows you to see the end product of the dream. Once you can see it, you can achieve it. Faith allows you to look beyond who you are to the one who created you and who knows you more than you know yourself. Faith allows you to keep your eyes on the prize even when all around you is crumbling. Faith takes you by the hand and restores your health, increases your finances, restores your broken home, and maximizes your potential. With God, all things are possible and He has already made the provisions for you to live a fulfilled and purposeful life.

3. ***Faith INITIATES actions***

Faith without works is dead. You can't say you have faith and refuse to give up complacency and go for what you want. Faith should mobilize you into action. You are hoping to pursue your degree but yet you sit down and do nothing. Do you think that you can sit down, do nothing, and achieve such? You will have to do something. I can hear you say, "I'll do it tomorrow," but tomorrow may be too late. Since you are sure of today, why not start now. Make use of the opportunities you have now. You need a job? Get your resume together and start sending them out to those places where you desire to work. You want to start your own business, start doing the research that will answer the questions of when, where, why, how. Remember if your faith is like a mustard seed, you can remove mountain.

4. ***Faith TRANSMITS power***

When faith is put to work, you will be saturated with a power you have never experienced before: power to overcome obstacles; power to reach for all that you could ever dream or image; power to transform a once impossible situation to possibility; power to rise above the expectations set by others; power to break an addiction; power to be the best that you can ever be. When faith is exercised, the powers in the universe move in your favor. Doors of opportunity start to open and things will never be the same again.

5. ***Faith produces HARD WORK***

For your dreams to be accomplished, you will have to decide to give it all you can. You may have to sacrifice the things that are dear to you; you may have to turn twenty-four hours into thirty-six; you may have to put your possessions in storage for a while. But one thing is sure, you must work hard. True success comes with hard work, and there is no real success without faith.

The Nature of Faith at Work

In 1998 a friend invited me to witness an agreement for her. She was buying a house in a new housing scheme in Jamaica. We were early and taken on a tour of the place by the developer of the scheme. I went into one particular house and fell in love with it, but, because of my financial situation at the time, knew I could not afford it. I remember standing and looking out through one of the windows with a clear view of the main road and the houses below. I said to myself, "I cannot afford to buy it, but I perhaps could rent it."

The developer asked me, "Do you want it to buy?"

My response was, "Yes, but I cannot afford it."

He then asked, "Are you a contributor of the National Housing Trust (NHT)?"

I said, "Yes, but I know nothing about it." The truth was, I thought the NHT was for low-income earners. Anyway, out of curiosity, I went to inquire. As a result of the information I received, my faith in the possibility of owning that home was activated. What seemed impossible the day before now seemed possible. My negative thoughts were no longer dominant. I started to focus my thoughts on that which was possible and saw myself as the new owner of the property. Consequently, my vision was amplified, and I could see the bigger picture of the steps I would need to take to make this dream a reality.

The NHT gave me a list of the things I would need to put together and take back to them, which included the surveyor's report, the valuator's report, and a receipt for a five-percent deposit. I never hesitated. I started to put my faith into action.

Was it easy? No! With no money in the bank to pay the five percent deposit, I started to ponder ways in which I could accumulate the sum of one hundred twenty-five thousand dollars. My faith was put to work. I got the money and was able to take the receipt to the NHT. As I said, it was not easy, but when you learn to trust God to provide for you, He will never let you down. Here, with hard work, there was a transformation of power. I moved from having a desire for this house to being the owner.

Once you recognize God's will in your life, you can remove mountains with your faith. James 4:3 tells us that, "Ye ask, and receive not, because ye ask amiss, that ye may consume it upon lust." Matthew 6:33 further says, "Seek ye first the kingdom of God and all His righteousness, then all other things shall be added unto you."

If you doubt in your heart, you cannot receive of the Lord. If the meteorologist told you that it was going to rain, then it would be unwise to go out without an umbrella. Since you do not want to get wet, you go out prepared. Similarly, if you expect anything from the Lord, you need to prepare yourself for it. As a matter of fact, God will not give you the blessing until you are fully prepared. Be on the alert and position yourself for your blessing.

Faith vs. Reason

Faith is having the confidence that we will receive that which we hoped for. It is the belief that we will receive, even when there is no evidence. Reason, on the other hand, looks for the evidence before activating belief.

The disciples were in the upper room hiding for fear of the Jews when Jesus appeared unto them. But doubtful Thomas did not believe that it was Jesus. He said in St. John 20:25, "Except I shall see in his hands the print of the nail, and put my finger into the print of the nails, and thrust my hand in his side, I will not believe." In verse 27, Jesus instructed him to do it and at that point, Thomas believed. Then Jesus said to him in verse 29,

"Thomas, because thou hast seen me, thou hast believed: blessed are they that have not seen, and yet have believed."

Reason relies on the senses for belief to take place. You look for it; you listen for it; you smell for it; you taste for it; and you feel for it. But when faith is at work, you see without seeing, you hear without hearing, you feel without feeling, you smell without smelling, and you taste without tasting. In other words, you will receive that which you hoped for even if you see nothing, hear nothing, smell nothing, taste nothing, and feel nothing.

When faith says you are healed, reason asks how you can be healed and yet are still feeling the pain. When faith says your dream of pursuing your education is possible, reason says how can this be, when you have no money. When faith says Mr. John is yours, reason says how can this be, when he is not even paying any attention to you. Reason always says the opposite of what faith says. Hebrews 11: 6 says, "But without faith it is impossible to please him: for he that cometh to God must believe that he is a rewarder of them that diligently seek him." So when faith tells you to trust God, to apply his healing power to your illness, do not allow reason to tell you that your sickness has reached too far, that you have only ten days to live. Look beyond the knowledge of the doctors to the one who is able to do all things. Look beyond your financial difficulties to the God who holds the wealth of this world in his hands. Look to the God who is able to transform the mind of your spouse, thus, creating a new person out of your spouse.

Exercising faith does not mean that the pathway will be smooth. As a matter of fact, that is farthest from the truth. There will be times when your faith will be put to the test. You will feel like nothing is working out, that you are wasting your time. But don't rely on your feelings. They are there to prevent you from reaching forward. Remember feelings don't last. You will feel this way today and tomorrow you will feel differently. Hold on to your faith, no matter what.

Make sure, however, that you are in the will of the Lord before you exercise faith. Because the truth is you may just receive that which is not the best for you. Whatever you focus on will become your reality. You may ask, "How can I be sure that I am in the will of God?" If what you desire to receive by faith is contradicting the word of God, then it is not His will. If you are not sure, ask God to reveal His will for that which you desire and trust Him to work it out for you. If it is His will, it will happen; if it is not His will, it will not happen. Trust His answer. He knows best. Faith produces patience, so you may have to wait for God's promises to come alive in your life. But no matter what, do not give up until you have received.

The disciples were in the boat when they saw Jesus walking on the water. At first they thought it was a ghost. But Peter said, "Lord, if it is you, bid me come to you." But as soon as he started to walk, he allowed reasoning to take over and he began to sink. But Jesus saved him and said, "Oh ye of little faith."

When God told Moses to stretch the rod across the Red Sea, no doubt reason was saying, "What can this do when the enemy is upon us?" But Moses knew that nothing was impossible with God and that it was important to obey the voice of God when He spoke. He stretched the rod across and the water divided.

Though reason told Job that God was angry with him and he would rather curse God and die, he did not succumb to reason; rather, he hung on to his faith. He said, "Though he slay me, yet will I serve him," and in the end Job was blessed tremendously.

The devil is aware of the blessings that God has in store for you and will try to put stumbling blocks in your path. Don't allow him to stop you from pursuing your dreams. Hold on to them and never let go. Stand firm in God and watch Him work in your life. He will go beyond reason and honor your faith with supernatural evidences.

Part Two

A Special You

Chapter Seven

You Are Special

> *But ye are a chosen generation, a royal priesthood, an holy nation, a peculiar people, that ye should shew forth the praises of him who hath called you out of darkness into his marvelous light.*
>
> 1 Peter 2:9

My imagination takes me back to the time of creation when God decided to create you. I can see Him shaping your every feature, implanting a magnitude of potentials and abilities, and selecting the family of which He wants you to be a part. He created you the way you are because that's how He wants you to be. Don't take this for granted; you were fearfully and wonderfully made and there is none upon the face of this earth like you. You are unique. You are chosen. You are peculiar. You are special. I often remind my children how unique and special they are. This is a fact I do not want them to forget. And neither should you.

When society throws its rags at you, remember you are special. When those you trusted abuse you in one form or another, remember you are special. When your spouse tells you how much he/she despises you, remember you are special. When the finances are low and you feel like giving up, remember you are special. When your burdens are too hard to bear, remember you are special.

Right where you are just now, you are there for a purpose. For God to use you the way He wants, He may need to shape you by teaching you about patience, long-suffering, humility, and devotion to Him. Paul said, "Whatever state I am in, therewith to be content." So don't be discouraged and don't despair. When you have reached that place God wants you to be, He will put you on higher ground.

Don't forget Moses. He spent forty years in the wilderness. God was preparing him to perform a special task, and a difficult task it was. But Moses was well-equipped. You see, God will not require of you what He knows you can't do. Whatever instructions He gives, it is because He knows you capable; you are special.

God does not waste time designing what is of no value to Him. He designed you and made you because you are special to Him. Hence, give Him the chance to work with you to bring out the special person you are. It is important to know who you are.

Who You Are Not

Before I tell you who you are, let me first tell you who you are not:

- ***You are not the color of your skin***. Whether you are white, black, red, or yellow, that's not who you are. The color of your skin is simply for identification. It is not for you to look up or down on yourself. Oh I am white, so I am superior; or I am black, so I'm inferior. If you were the color of your skin, then you would be nothing. When sickness or old age stepped in, you would surely not know who you were. You have a jar of the same kind of candies and, though they are wrapped in varying colored paper, they are the same candies. The color does not make them any better. They contain the same ingredients. It's the same with us. We were all made from the dust of the earth. Hence, though we may be different nations with different colors, we are one. We are the same. The color of our skin does not define who we are. You are not the color of your skin.

- ***You are not the sum total of what you have acquired***. Many of us lost our identities because we think of ourselves as being the things we acquired over the years. When finances get low and the brand names are no longer affordable, we start to think that life is not worth living. When we can't afford the luxurious vacations we are used to, then we think it's time to give up. If what we possess is who we are, then we would be nothing. If we can't drive luxurious cars like our neighbors, we begin to think of ourselves as nobody. Hence, in order to feel like somebody, we cheat, steal, and kill. The recession of 2009 taught us the valuable lesson that we are not what we have. A friend said to me during this time that it is foolish to think of ourselves as what we have acquired. And that is why we should never look down on the man who has less than we have, as one day we might very well find ourselves in his category. I have seen people who were really making it come to nothing because they were once defined by what they had.
- ***You are not the community you live in.*** Although studies have shown that the environment of which we are a part determines to a large extent who we are, you are not defined by the community of which you a part. You may be living in a poor community where there is a high level of crime and violence and one in which little emphasis is placed on education or good moral values. This does not mean that you can't achieve anything in life, and it certainly does not stop

you from being the best that you can ever be. There is much evidence telling you that you can live above your present situation. You are not the community of which you are a part.

> Jesus was a Nazarene and the question was asked, "Can any good come out of Nazareth?" Too often I have heard the comment, "Oh, he is from community x so he can't do any better." That's a lie the devil wants you to believe, but don't fall for his cunningness. He is a deceiver and always will be, so don't fall for his tricks. You are not the community of which you are a part.
>
> When I was in secondary school, we were made to believe that no good could come out of a particular community, and I believed all the people there were cruel and wicked. So when it was announced that the head girl was from that community, I said to myself, *Can that happen?* Yes, it did. If you think life will never be better for you, the truth is, if that's what you think, that is exactly what you will get.

- ***You are not the job you do.*** Many people coming to the United States of America, though professionally trained in their native land, choose to do mediocre jobs because of their immigration status. But whether you have to give up your prestigious job for a lower category, or whether you move from the position of an executive secretary to that of an office cleaner, you are not the job you do. It does not define you. It does not make you any less than you are. People who are defined by the job they do are the ones who will soon forget who they are.

They are the ones who will refuse to do anything worthwhile for the sake of surviving. You are not the job you do.

- ***You are not the clothes you wear.*** Clothes play a part in making us feel good or bad about ourselves, but they do not define who we are. One person says, "I am behind my face. I am behind what I wear." Whether you are dressed elegantly or not, you are not the clothes you wear. My friend was walking behind a beautifully dressed woman, and a part of her dress was messed up. My friend touched her to inform her of the mess, only to be attacked by the woman, who, of course, was mentally disturbed! How many times have we seen people dressed in shabby apparel and the first thought that came to our minds is *that's a poor person,* only to discover that the truth covered in those poor shabby garments is a beautiful, educated, God-fearing person! You are not what you wear.

Who Are You?

Now that you know who you are not, let me tell you exactly who you are. ***You are God's special handmaiden***. My mom, being a dressmaker, always comes up with beautiful designs. One design was a green dress she made with the skirt pleated, and then steam pressed, which was done manually with a self-heater iron that used coal to produce the heat.

My mother took special care to make sure the dress came out the way she desired it. She followed a step-by-step process. Similarly, when God decided to create you, He made note of all the details, as He intended you to come out a perfect creation. Can you see Him with a smile on his face as He bent over to carve you into existence? No wonder when He was finished He looked and said, "That's good."

After a number of years, I can still hear the voice of the late Mr. Archer as he sang *From the dust of the earth God created man, In his likeness he created man a living soul***.**

Can you imagine the joy that God felt when He came up with that special design of you? Your physical features—whether you'll be tall or short, black or white, fat or slim, long hair or short hair, brown eyes or dark eyes, and so on.

You are not an afterthought of God. You are God's special masterpiece. He took everything about you into account. He even knows the number of hairs on your head! The psalmist reminds us in Psalms 139:14, "I will praise thee for I am fearfully and wonderfully made: marvelous are thy works and my soul knoweth right well."

Hence, when the temptation comes to compare yourself with others and to envy others for who they are, remember that you are specially designed to be who you are. So thank God for the knock-knees and the short hair; thank him for the broad nose and the big ear.

You are so special to God that, even when at creation you disobeyed Him and could have been destroyed, He sent the only son He had to die for you so that you can have life once again and have it in abundance.

Though you erred and caused Him great embarrassment so many times, He never disowned you. Instead He made provision for you to have your sins forgiven. He sent Jesus Christ as your advocate. So don't give up on yourself when things are not going well. Trust God to work things out for you. Don't take on the cares of this life that will throw you into deep depression. Taking on too much will sometimes make you feel like committing suicide. Give your burdens to Jesus. He cares much for you. If you will allow Him, He will be your all-in-all: your Savior, your friend, your counselor, your provider, your protector, your everything. He will never disappoint you. You are His special handmaiden, and He cares for you.

You are a part of a royal family. How often have you thought that if only you were a part of the Jones family everything would be okay? But you know what, if God intended for you to be a part of the Jones family, He would have put you there. But the purpose He has for you will not be accomplished by being a part of the Jones family. He put you where you are because that's where He wants you to be. You are forgetting that you are of a part of a family that is much more mighty and powerful than the Joneses. You are a part of the royal family! You are special! You are royalty!

Jesus Christ, the King of this earth, calls you His brother. So how dare you look down on yourself and think you are a nobody. Rise up and be all that God wants you to be. Did He make you an underachiever? No! Did He create you to make drugs the master of your life? No! Did He create you to let men use and abuse you? No! He created you to claim your position in the royal family and be all that He intends you to be.

Don't give in to low self-esteem, poor self-concept, poverty, underachievement, an unfulfilled life, or failure in your life. Claim all the blessings that God has in store for you. Get up like the prodigal boy and say, "I will go unto my father."

Don't stay in a state of self-defeat and self-pity. One of the things I hate to hear people say is, "Poor me." Since what you say is what you get, you need to start saying, "Rich me."

Though right now you may be sitting in a wheelchair, unable to move like you used to, don't feel sorry for yourself. You are of a part of a royal family and God can use you to accomplish a lot right where you are.

A former supervisor I had never thought he would be in a wheelchair today. He could have been killed when he was shot, but God preserved his life and instead put him in a wheelchair. Today he is spreading the good news of salvation from his chair. He claimed his position in the royal family in spite of his circumstances. You need to do the same.

You are God's chosen. Man's general purpose on earth is to serve God, but each of us is given a special task that God wants us to accomplish. In other words, we are chosen. To be more specific, you are chosen. Did you know that no matter what you go through in life you are chosen for such? Do you remember the story of Job? The devil could not put his hands on Job until God gave him permission. But the truth is, if God had known that Job could not pass the test, He would not have allowed him to go through it. God knew Job better than Job knew himself. Job was chosen.

When the road gets rough and the waves of life toss you to and fro, remember you are chosen only because you have it in you to succeed, to pass the test. The devil will try to convince you that there is no way out, that it is better to kill your family and then commit suicide. But look him in the eyes and remind him that he is a professional liar and you will never believe anything he says. He has been a deceiver from the beginning of time, and his sole purpose is to destroy you as he was destroyed. Get up and go to your father, for you are chosen. He will give you the strength you need to live a victorious life.

The bank account may be drained, but you were chosen for that. You may have lost the home you had invested in, but you were chosen for that. You may have lost dear family members in an accident, but you were chosen for that. Your business may have been bankrupted, but you were chosen for that. You are chosen only because you are special to God. So in the midst of your trial, give God the praise for choosing you and continue to walk in faith. You are chosen.

You are the only one like you. As a grade seven coordinator, it was my responsibility to place students in various grade-seven classes. During the process, however, sometimes mistakes were made where twins were separated and placed in different classes or placed on different shifts. In one such situation, two girls who were identical were placed on separate shifts. I was not aware of this until one day in my math class, I saw a girl outside who I thought should be in my class. I was on the first shift then. I remember moving towards the door and I asked the student what she was doing outside. To my surprise, the students became hysterical. I was curious and asked, "What are you laughing at?"

One student answered, "Miss, it's not her. It is her sister." I looked at the back of the class and saw the other sister staring at me amused. It was then that I discovered the sisters were identical. Can you imagine how surprised I was! Even though they were identical, I watched each girl and, as time went by, differences could be seen in their whole mannerism and attitude towards work.

And so it is with you. You are the only you. There is no one who is like you. Everyone has his or her unique identity. No two people have the same fingerprint. Isn't that amazing? Though you may wear the same ring size, your fingerprints are different! That's how unique you are. Because of that fact, you must learn to accept you for who you are; that is, your strengths and weaknesses, your physical beauty or ugliness, your capability or incapability. Never compare yourself with anyone, as you may end up feeling inferior or superior—both extremes are dangerous. If you can't accept yourself for who you are, then you will not be able to accept others for who they are.

Ask God to help you to accept those things that can't be changed and to change those things that can be changed. He won't let you down as He too knows the importance of accepting oneself.

For a great portion of my life, I thought I was tall in stature until I went to college and met Cheryl, who became my roommate and good friend. She was short, and I used to brag that I was taller than she was. One day on our way to the cafeteria, we were arguing about who was taller. A fellow colleague heard us and asked what we were arguing about. After a while he said to us, "You can stop arguing, as both of you are short!" We were hysterical.

I now accept the fact that I am short. If God wanted me to be tall then I would be tall. He has a purpose for my shortness even if it meant asking Cheryl, the taller of us (she still thinks that way), to go for the plate bag when I was too lazy to go for it.

Don't forget for a moment how unique and special you are. Don't forget that you are from a royal family and that you were specially chosen. Hold your head up high and give God praise for creating you the way you are. Use your uniqueness to bringing honor and glory to your creator.

The Visible You

Do people see the real you or do they see the you that you pretend to be? Jesus says in Matthew 5:16 (AV), "Let your light so shine before men that they may see your good works and glorify your father which is in heaven."

Now that you know who you are and who you are not, live like who you are that others may emulate you; that they may want to be like you. Be an example in everything you do. Live worthy of your name. When it is being called, let the sound of dignity and strong character echo.

Stop underestimating who you are and what you can do. Make the sky your limit. Be all that you can ever be. Walk hand-in-hand with your designer and don't give Him reason to regret making you.

In Colossians 4:17 (AV) it says, "And whatever you do in word or deed, do all in the name of the Lord Jesus, giving thanks to God and father by him." Let others see the Christ living in you. Let them want to be in your presence at all times. When Jesus was on earth, he would have multitudes following him because of who he was.

"Let your speech be always seasoned with grace, that he may know how he ought to answer every man." (Col. 4:6, AV) Stay away from gossip. Let your words be words of wisdom; words that will encourage others to be the best that they can ever be.

And don't forget to seek God's kingdom first. Let God be the master of your life. I know it is easier said than done, but God will give you the strength. He will not ask you to do something He knows is impossible for you to do.

Be the visible you. If you don't accept yourself for who you are then it will be hard for others to accept you.

The story is told of the little boy who went climbing in the mountains and found an eagle's nest with eggs in it. When he got home, he put one of the eggs under a hen with her eggs. When the eagle hatched, he thought he was a chicken. As a result, he learned chicken behavior and scratched in the chicken yard with his siblings as he did not know any better. But sometimes he felt strange stirrings within himself, but did not know what to do with them. He thought to himself that as a chicken he should act like a chicken.

One day an eagle flew over the chicken yard and the young eagle looked up and saw him. Suddenly he longed to be like that eagle. He wanted to fly high in the mountains. And then as he spread his wings, he realized he was like that eagle. Although he had never flown before, he realized that he had the capability and instinct to do so. At his first trial, he was a bit unsteady, but with more practice he became better at it. With time, the eagle became what he was created to be. And so it is with you. You too can fly high in the mountain. You can be all that God wants you to be. You can be the visible you. You don't have to continue to pretend to be who you are not. Soon the coat of pretense will fall and others will see you for who you really are.

Challenge yourself to be somebody that others will love and respect. Maximize your potential and be the special person that God created you to be. "Lying lips are abomination to the Lord:" (Prov. 12:22, AV) Live the truth of who you really are and watch God work in your life. You will make mistakes in life, and you will make decisions which will affect you for the rest of your life, but that does not mean you are not important to God.

A poor parent you may be, but to God you are important; a prostitute you may be, but to God you are important; unattractive you may be, but to God you are important; a drug addict you may be, but to God you are important; an alcoholic you may be, but to God you are important. All He is asking you to do is to take your shattered past to him, and He will put you back on the path you should be on. That's how important you are to Him.

God knows that somewhere in life you will become discouraged and downhearted, and for that He has made the provision, "Come unto me all ye that labor, and are heavy laden, and I will give you rest." (Matt. 11:28, AV) Be the you God created you to be and be happy for who you are.

Chapter Eight

You Are Just as Important

Be not afraid, for I have ransomed you. I have called you by name; you are mine.

Isaiah. 43:1

Being the only female tenor in the Challengers Gospel Band, my attendance at rehearsals was very important. Every member of the group had a significant role, and replacement due to absence was difficult. Similarly, now that God has placed you where you are and has equipped you with the necessary tools needed to accomplish that which He intends for you to do, you need to stop thinking of yourself as unimportant or insignificant, for you are not. You are important.

The human tendency is to compare ourselves with others, and when we are not able to do what they can do, we think we are not important. The office cleaner in a company is just as important as the CEO in the company. They all work towards the betterment of the company and the work environment.

The body gives a good illustration as to how important you are in the whole process of God's creation. Though each has a distinct function, all the body parts are important. If the eyes stop working, then the entire body is affected; if the feet stop working, then the entire body is affected. Why? Because each body part is just as important as another.

It is hoped that by the end of this chapter you will cease comparing yourself with others. Thank God for who you are, and make who you are a great contributor to making this world a better place.

To God You Are Important

While he was on earth Jesus associated himself with the outcasts of society: the man with leprosy, the prostitute, and the tax collectors. But though society looked down on them, Jesus saw the treasure lying beneath them. He saw their worth; he saw the gold that was ready to be refined and, as a result, He spared time to reach out to them. "He came to seek and to save that which was lost." He came to "preach good tidings unto the meek, to bind up the brokenhearted, to proclaim liberty to the captives, and to open the prison to them that are bound."

As I have discussed before, at creation you were God's special design. He equipped you with talents and abilities to accomplish the purpose you have here an earth. But perhaps you have lost focus and become busy doing things that were not meant for you—trying to play the guitar when you have no knack for music may not be a good idea. Know your strengths and weaknesses. That's the only way to determine what you were created to do. And you may never know until you've tried.

You are right where you are at this particular moment, in this particular place, because that's where you ought to be.

Because you are important to God, sometimes you will be tested by fire so that you can be as pure gold in order to accomplish your task. You are important to God, and that's why He created you the way you are. So stop complaining, murmuring, and longing to be like your mom or your best friend, because the truth is you can never be them. You are unique.

I have always admired ladies with nicely shaped legs and have wished that mine could be that way, too. But if God intended me to have nicely shaped legs, He would have given them to me. Like Apostle Paul, I have learned that "in whatever state I am therewith to be content."

I pity the ladies who are not satisfied with the color of their skin and try to bleach themselves. They think that the browner they are, the more beautiful they will be or the more they will be accepted by society, and, of course, the more one is accepted by society, the more value one places upon himself or herself.

I remember when I was teaching at Anchovy High School, a young lady in one of my senior classes was obviously not satisfied with the color of her skin, so she bleached her face and left the rest of her body untouched. A young man passing the classroom saw her and shouted, "Miss Vassell, why do you allow a monkey in your class?" I tried to keep a straight face, but the entire class was hysterical.

None of us is perfect. We make wrong decisions and live our lives filled with regrets, but that does not mean we are not important to God. A poor parent you may be, but to God you are important. You may have failed many times, but to God you are important. You may be living on the street, but to God you are important. You may have been classified as an outcast, but to God you are important. You will have to see the treasure you are and accept the fact that you are important.

Can you imagine that you are so important to God that after you fell from His grace, He sent his only son, Jesus Christ, to die for you so that your relationship with Him could be restored? To further show how important you are to God, He says in Matthew 6:25, "Therefore I say unto you, take no thought for your life, what ye shall eat, or what ye shall drink; or for your body, what ye shall put on. Is not life more than meat and the body more than raiment? Behold the fowls of the air; for they sow not, neither do they reap, nor gather into barns, yet your Heavenly Father feedeth them. Are ye not much better than they?"

So stop feeling sorry for yourself. Stop taking on the weight of this world. Stop trying to be somebody else. Stop making drugs and alcohol the master of your life; stop accepting abuse, for that is not God's plan for your life. You are too important to God to be living a mediocre, unfulfilled life. *Rise up and walk* is God's command to you. It's not the end of the world. God loves you and you will always be important to him.

Life Would Never Be the Same without You.

I don't care what your fate is in life; the truth is that life would never be the same without you. Your role is just as important as that of your friends or any family member. The space you occupy right now is yours. It is called self-space and is significant to the rest of the space around you.

In baking a black cake for Christmas, as is a Jamaican tradition, the recipe has to be followed carefully for the cake to turn out well. The butter, the eggs, the sugar, and all other ingredients are important, though each serves a different purpose. Forget to put in the right number of eggs or amount of baking powder and your cake will not be the black cake you wish it to be.

This world is made up of different tribes and races, and each plays an important role. Think of the world without the Asians or the Blacks, the world would never be the same. Having gone to the Penn Relays in Philadelphia year after year, I discovered that the stadium is vastly populated by Jamaicans. Without them, the relays would not be the same. And so it is with you, the universe would never be the same without you.

You do not have to be a Paris Hilton, an Obama, or a Rodriquez to be important. The little part that you may play makes you just as important. If everybody wore white-colored suits, what do you think would happen?

Since the death of my grandmother, our family has never been the same. Going to the family home in the country is not the same. Grandma was the pillow that held the family together. Most of the time, everyone went to the country because of her. Now that she has gone home to be with her Savior, visits are rare.

You may not be where God wants you to be; you may not be doing the job you want to do; you may not find the man/woman you wish to be your mate; you may not be singing in the choir as you wish; you may not have yet achieved your educational goals, but don't forget for one moment that you are important and the world would never be the same without you.

Pause right where you are right now. You may be on the verge of giving up; you may feel that life is not worth living after your partner walked out on you; you may feel like all is lost since you no longer have a job; you may think that committing suicide is your answer to your problem, but, my dear friend, God understands all that you are going through, and He is waiting with out-stretched arms to relieve you of the burden that presses you down. Give it to Him. He knows that your mission in this world is not yet accomplished. He knows that the world will never be the same without you. Your friends need you, your family needs you, and God needs you. So don't give up.

It was in the year 1996 that I felt that my burdens were too hard to bear. I walked to the refrigerator on which stood the bottle of iron tablets. I poured some in my hand, then they moved to my mouth, but it was not to be. That was not the solution to my problem. That experience helped me to understand the value of life, and how important it is for us to live our lives the way God wants us to. If I were successful in doing what I intended to do, my daughters would have no mom around. Then life for them would never be the same.

Now you know that you are important and that life would never be the same without you, live like you are important.

Live like You Are Important

By now you may have established what your purpose in life is and now is the time to live like you are important. I do not mean that you should go around thinking too highly of yourself, drawing attention to yourself, but instead, in your humble little corner, be the best that you can ever be and aim at having a positive influence on the lives of those you come in contact with. Let others long to meet you again.

Some years ago, I read a book entitled *What Would Jesus Do?*, and I realized that if this question is consistently asked in our lives, then life would never be the same. We would have better control of ourselves and enact a positive influence on the lives of others. When our children cause us pain, the answer to 'What would Jesus do' will allow us to control our anger and make us more understanding. I am not saying that it is easy, but I think it is a better remedy than counting to ten.

The only way to live your life as if you are important is to let the mind that was in Christ Jesus be in you. Do not forget what you have learned in the earlier chapters in this book. We are our own thoughts. Living your live in false humility will not do it. All it will do is draw attention to you. It's as if you are saying, "Look at me. Don't you see how humble I am?" Jesus left the beauty of heaven and came and lived as a humble servant. He chose to put the feelings of others ahead of his own. His disciples loved to be in his presence.

Whatever your mission in life, do it as unto the Lord and not men. Hence, when you play the piano, you will do it to the best of your ability. When you are at work, you will not only do your best when your boss is around, but will thrive to do your best at all times and I am sure, very positive, that you will be rewarded. Not only will others learn to trust you, but you may receive a salary increase or promotion that you least expected.

When you have tried to bring your dream to fruition and have failed, tell yourself that you are too important to give up. When the mortgage gets so high that your house may go in foreclosure, tell yourself that you are too important to let this get you down. You are there because of your importance. You would not have been there if you were not equipped with the strength and the wisdom to go through it. It may be winter now, but your springtime is just ahead.

No problem lasts forever and for every problem there is a solution. Somebody says, "If you are going through hell, keep going." Don't walk around with a frown on your face. Strive to appear the best that you can ever be. Wash your face and add a little make-up if necessary. Feel lifted on the inside and it will confuse the enemy.

A friend who knew the problems I was facing at a particular time in my life, asked me one day, "Maizie, how do you look so well with everything you are going through?"

My response to her was, "I put out extra effort to confuse the devil. I want him to be disappointed in his effort to keep me down!" My trials are to test my faith, and I shall come forth stronger than before, because I am important to God.

For example, a woman thought the least of herself when her spouse walked out on her. She may have thought it was the end of life; hence, she gave up on herself. No more fancy hairdos, no more tailored suits. But a spouse walking out is sometimes not a bad thing as you will get the chance to be who God intended you to be! The word of God says, "In everything give thanks."

And likewise, men, don't be disappointed when women walk out of your life. Maybe you were not meant to be together. It's not the end of the world! Turn over all your disappointments to the One who promised to be your burden bearer. You can do it. He will give you the strength. There is absolutely nothing that God can't do for you. Trust Him to work things out for you, to be your best, for you are important, and should live life as though you are important.

Chapter Nine

Use Your God Given Ability

And he gave some apostles; and some prophets; and some evangelists; and some, pastors and teachers.

Ephesians 4:11

One day I was talking to a friend who said she wished she had special talents and abilities. She did not think God had given her any. But my response to her was that God created every man for a special purpose and to each he gives unique talents and abilities. They are there, but it's for her to discover them.

One of the problems we face as humans is having the tendency to compare ourselves with others and then begrudging them for what they have. We say, "If only I could sing like Beyoncé or I wish I could write poems like Tom." But God did not intend for you to use somebody else's ability. He intended for you to use that which He has given you. If you were not given the ability to sing, be satisfied with that; if you did not get the ability to lead, then stop trying to prove yourself and leave it to who was given that ability. If you were called to preach, then preach; if you were called to teach, then teach.

The church is comprised of people with different talents and abilities. Not everyone was called to be a deacon; not everyone was called to be an evangelist. Spend time to find what your special abilities are and work to improve them. The more you use them, the better they'll be. The Apostle Paul says, "And he gave some, apostles; and some prophets; and some evangelists; and some, pastors and teachers."

The bottom line is, no matter your talents and abilities they were given to you by God to bring Him glory. Hence, if they are used otherwise, then it is safe to say, they are being misused. True success can only come your way when you learn to use these God-given talents and abilities to bring honor to God.

Use the Little You Have

Moses said (paraphrased), God, how can you ask me to go and talk to Pharaoh when you know that I'm a man of slow speech? But look at the job he performed! He led the children of Israel out of Egypt. He did an excellent job and even though he never saw the Promised Land, that does not take from the fact that he performed well.

You are given a little, but your little can create miracles; it can remove mountains; it can bring joy where sadness once existed. Use the little you have. You may not be able to preach a sermon, but when you encourage somebody to a better way of life, then you have done much. You may not be as educated as your friend, but you can do much with what you have.

David was not a trained soldier but he used the little he had to conquer Goliath. He said, "You come to me with a sword but I come to you in the name of the Lord."

Dr. Stephen Grellef, a former French Quaker Missionary said, "I shall pass through this world once. If therefore there is any kindness I can show, or any good thing I can do, let me do it now; let me not defer it or neglect it for I shall not pass this way again." Use the little you have now, as you may never get the chance to use it again, and what a waste that would be!

If you take the little you have and use it to the best of your ability, you will be surprised to see what you can achieve. Because of ill health, my younger sister did not complete high school. But that has not stopped her from using the abilities God has given her. She is blessed with artistic abilities and, though she may not be as good as other professional artists, she uses the little she has to create cards for someone on Mother's or Father's day. People love her creative, old-English writing and order framed work from her. In bringing joy to someone's mother or father, she in turn has become joyous.

If you have the ability to create a beautiful environment for worship, use it. Do it for the Lord and not men and you will be surprised at the blessings you will bring to others.

You Are Not Too Old to Be Used

"Let the young people do it as I am too old now."

"I'm too old to go back to school. God will soon be coming to take charge of his world so I can't be bothered."

"Anything can happen, let it happen."

These are some of the most destructive thoughts one can ever entertain. Let me remind my old friends that age is just a number. I have been encouraging friends and relatives to pursue their education and they often remind me that going to college for, perhaps, another four years is a total waste of time. But now, looking back after four years have passed when they would have been finished, they say, "If I had only known—." Now it is harder, as they have assumed more responsibilities and have less time.

When God promised Abraham and Sarah a son, they thought they were too old and had almost lost confidence in the fact that with God nothing is impossible. If God has placed something in your heart for you to do, don't think that you can't do it because you are too old. I have heard of cases where people pursue their high school diploma at age seventy! Grandma Lee was seventy-five years old when she competed in *America's Got Talent* and made it to the finals. What if she had sat down because she thought she was too old?

Elderly folks in the churches today have the tendency to lay down arms, thinking they have already done their part. But the truth is, God is not through with you yet no matter how old you are. Though your youthful energy may be depleted, there is still energy to accomplish that which God desires you to achieve. He promised never to leave you nor forsake you. And He will give you the strength and the wisdom to do it. I have seen elderly people, who, in spite of pain, visit restaurants at least three times during the week, but use the same pain as an excuse for not going to church.

Retirement does not mean retirement from God. It can mean doing more for God that you were not able to do when you were employed. It may mean being present at Bible study. Do not allow your age to get in the path of God using you to fulfill the purpose for which you were created. Paul says in Romans 8: 35-39:

> Who shall separate us from the love of Christ? Shall tribulation, or distress, or persecution, or famine, or nakedness, or peril, or sword? As it is written, for thy sake we are killed all day long, we are accounted as sheep for the slaughter. Nay in all these things, we are more than conquerors through him that loved us. For I am persuaded, that neither death, nor life, nor angels, nor principalities, nor powers, nor things present, nor things to come, nor heights, nor depth, nor any other creature shall be able to separate us from the love of God, which is in Christ Jesus our Lord.

Do you know how old Moses was when God called him to lead the children of Israel out of Egypt? Moses was eighty years old! Most of you may have thought God unreasonable; that Moses was too old to be used. But in spite of his age, Moses did it anyhow. “The race is not for the swift but for they that endured to the end.”

So stop right where you are. If you are not on the path of success for God, then you need to turn around and step on the pedal of success. Think young and you will feel young. A former principal at my school never saw himself older than twenty-five, even when he was in his late fifties, and what an energy he emanates!

Commit your ailment to God who is able to soothe the pain and suffering of the human race. Do you know that sometimes the pain is as a result of our thoughts?

Ask God for the strength and the courage that you need to make it to the end, and at the end, you will hear "Well done thou good and faithful servant—."

Who Says You Are Too Young to Be Used

When I was in third form in secondary school, I felt the need to give my life to God. It was not an easy decision as I was still young and wanted to enjoy the world a little bit more. My mother and pastor were there with me all the way. The path to this new life was rough and tough and many times I felt like giving up. I had to quit friendships and as a result was labeled *Miss Goody-Goody*. At first I thought that it was unfair to be labeled this way when all I wanted was to maintain a good relationship with the Lord.

God's favor was on me, and I could see progressive improvement in every area of my life. At age fifteen, I was elected President of the ISCF (Inter School Christian Fellowship) at school. I felt elated knowing that I was helping others to develop a better relationship with the Lord. By age twenty-four, I served in several offices in church—Sunday school teacher, secretary of the youth fellowship, clerk of the church—and even today I experience the blessings of the Lord. You are not too young to be used by God.

The psalmist declared in Psalms 119: 9-12 (NLT), "How can a young person stay pure? By obeying your word. I have tried hard to find you. Don't let me wander from your commands. I have hidden your word in my heart that I might not sin against you. I praise you, oh Lord, teach me your decrees."

When God calls you in your youth, He has great work for you to do. "Young men, I called upon you because you are strong." God wants you both for your physical strength as well as for your spiritual strength, but "Wherewithal shall a young man cleanse his way by taking heed thereto according to thy word." For you to make yourself available unto God, you have to feed your thoughts on the word of God and let it fill you richly. David says, "Thy word is a lamp unto my feet and a light unto my path." (Psa. 119:105) You are not too young to walk in the path that God wants you to walk.

Samuel was only twelve years old when God called him to prophesy. You might know the story, how in his sleep he heard someone calling him and thought that it was Eli the Priest. But after the second time, Eli realized that it must be God who was calling him; so he told Samuel that if he should hear the voice again he should say, "Speak lord for thy servant heareth." Samuel responded to the voice of the Lord and was used in a mighty way. Eli was warned of his son's evil through Samuel; David was anointed King through him as well. If you should hear God calling you today, harden not your heart. You are not too young to be used by God.

How old do you think David was when he slew Goliath? He was a teenager somewhere between sixteen and eighteen years old! He was the youngest of Jesse's sons. But did you know before that God allowed him to use his hands to kill a bear? (1 Sam. 17: 34-37) God was preparing him for the task ahead. So no matter how rough the road may be, God is preparing you for the work he has called you to do.

Daniel was only ten years old when he was taken into captivity in Babylon. But there, God used him and his young friends to service by allowing the King to find favor in them. Daniel was about fifteen years old when he refused to eat the unclean meat of the pagan King. He did it to please God and was awarded with great wisdom. As a matter of fact, he and his friends were found to be ten times wiser than the wise men in the King's realm. This could not have happened if they were not in touch with God. Daniel prayed at least three times a day. To be in touch with God, you have to be prayerful. You have to trust him to lead you on the path that you are to go. When God calls you into service, He will equip you with all that is necessary to complete the task. You may have been called to set the captives free; to put families back together; to free the drug addict from the harmful effects of drugs; to change the lives of those living promiscuously; to eradicate the mind of negative, self-defeating thoughts; and to create a path of resilience to those who are living in self-doubt, guilt, and on the verge of giving up.

If God is calling you today, don't hesitate to respond to the call. Don't say, "Not now; tomorrow I will." Get up and start working now. Esau lost his inheritance because he treated it as a small thing, and though he later repented, it was too late. Don't let this happen to you. Who says you are too young to be used? Use your God-given talents and abilities to bring sunshine and rays into the lives of others.

Chapter Ten

To Be Inferior Is Your Choice

So God created human beings in his image. In the image of God he created them male and female he created them.

Genesis 1:27

Growing up in semi-poverty, I oftentimes wished that life was not so hard. I longed to live in a better home and for my parents to be more financially stable. They tried as hard as they could to make sure that we were well taken care of. My mom would find all the possible ways to assist my father to bring in extra income for the family.

This longing created deficiency in my self-image. I allowed self-destructive thoughts to determine the image I have of myself. I compared myself with others who were enjoying a luxuriant life. I guess I can blame a little on society that cultured us into thinking of ourselves in the light of what we have acquired in life and the label given to us by others, whether it be negative or positive.

During my teen years, I overheard a relative comparing my cousin and me. It was said that my cousin has a better figure than I had, however I had a prettier face. Acquiring a handsome figure was what I had always hoped for, so can you imagine the negative effect this had on me then. I started thinking little of myself and, as somebody would say, I developed the grasshopper complex.

During those years, I did not realize that to be inferior was my choice. I was the one who chose to allow negative comments to dominate my thoughts.

No one can make you feel bad about yourself unless you allow it. I don't care what part of town you are from or if you are an underachiever, the thoughts you process in your mind are yours and yours alone and are controlled by you. You decide what you want to keep and what you must reject. It is hoped that at the end of the chapter you will learn to take control of what you believe about yourself and not what others want or wish you to believe.

You Are Not What They Say You Are

We are programmed to put things in categories: rich or poor, black or white, little or big, fat or slim, pretty or ugly, success or failure, educated or uneducated. As a result, we do not see the oneness in us or the universe in general.

Earlier in this book, I spoke about labels that we give to others and the effects they have on their self-image. But I want to reemphasize the fact that no one has the authority to put you anywhere. The only one with that authority is the God who created you, thus, you should only see yourself in the light of what He created you to be. You are not what people say you are; you are what you believe yourself to be.

It took a long while for me to comprehend and program myself into the belief that I have a choice whether to accept what others say about me as Gospel or to accept who I am in relation to who God says I am. It is our tendency to build our self-image on what we have achieved in life, but as I have discussed before, we are not the things we have acquired in life, nor are we the labels that we have been given. We are God's perfect creation. We are neither pretty nor ugly, we are who we are. We are His image. Have you forgotten that God looked on His perfect creation and said, "That's good?" So stop believing the lies others desperately want you to believe about yourself; stop putting yourself down. When you disregard your positive qualities for the negatives that others want you to believe about yourself, you will always have verification of what you're looking for.

Dr. Richard Carlson says:

> Putting yourself down reinforces rather than corrects your imperfections by placing unnecessary attention and energy on everything that's wrong, rather than what's right with you. Why should you do this knowing the only possible result is a negative outlook, more negative feelings, and less appreciation for the gift of life? People who regularly put themselves down are often seen as complainers, not to mention the examples they set. Everyone has aspects of themselves they'd like to improve, but this doesn't mean you should beat yourself up. Here on earth none of us is ever going to be perfect, but putting yourself down isn't the answer.

It's a pity, but not everyone wishes the best for you. There are those who labeled you so that they can have a job. There are those who labeled you because they think themselves higher than you, and still there are those who are envious of your potentials and abilities. There are those who consistently want to control your life. Stay away from those friends who never commend you. They always criticize and refuse to recognize improvement when it is staring them in the eyes.

When Paul told us in Romans 12:3 not to think of ourselves more highly than we ought to think, he was not asking us to feel less of ourselves. He was not telling us not to feel good about ourselves. In other words, low self-esteem was not what he had intended us to achieve, but rather that we should not put ourselves where we are not. He encouraged us to think of ourselves in accordance with the gift we have been given. Hence, if you were not given the gift of teaching, then don't strive to be a teacher, or if you were not given the talent to sing, then don't strive to be a singer. For those of us who watched *American Idol*, we can understand.

God created you the way you are because that's how He wanted you to be. Accept those things that you cannot change, but nothing is wrong with you changing the things that you can.

I was surprised one day when I got on the scale and found out that I had gained five pounds! I am sure a lot of ladies can identify with this. Yes, I may weigh a bit more than I want, but the truth is my body is not who I am. For health reasons and for the sake of avoiding a new wardrobe, I know I want to take off the extra five pounds.

You are a unique being and should not be compared with anyone. So my encouragement to parents is that they should not compare their children to others especially when it is done in their presence. These little ones have not yet acquired the skill of eliminating unwanted information and will believe what you say about them. So if you tell your child that he is a good-for-nothing, then that child is going to grow up thinking that he is a good-for-nothing. I have two daughters, and I use every opportunity to let them know how beautiful they are. They are not what people say they are; they were made in the wonderful image of God.

I was told once that I am an educated fool because I strive to improve my education. This person was trying to let me feel bad about myself, but I did not give him the chance, and, likewise, you should not give anyone such opportunity either.

The disciples thought the prostitute to be an outcast or a good-for-nothing. To avoid contradiction, and because Jesus saw worth in her, he sent the disciples away. Throughout his ministry on earth, Jesus associated himself with folks who appeared valueless to others. He knew people inside out and knew that man was created with value. People have only lost track of who they are. Jesus knows your worth. He knows your value. He knows your truest potential. He knows that you can be all that you were created to be.

Stop putting yourself down because of what your family, friend, teacher, or spouse said about you. You are wonderful; you are who you are no matter what they say you are. See yourself for the value God placed on you. Pull out all the rich resources you are blessed with. Strive to be your best at all times. Ask God to help you to accept who you are and to help you to fulfill the purpose for which you were created. You don't have to be a murderer; you don't have to use drugs to feel high; you should not continue to live a worthless life because of what people say you are. The power of what you want to be is in your hands. God is with you and will help you to overcome the negative image you have had about yourself for all these years. You are partnered with God. Work with Him to achieve all you hope to achieve for you are not what they say you are.

You Are behind Your Face

Do you think that anyone has the authority to criticize you as ugly? No one has that authority unless you give it to them. God made you the way you are because that's how he wants you to be. The media presents beauty as one's outward appearance: beautiful face, beautiful figure. But the truth is that you never should you see yourself for what you look like, but rather for who you are on the inside. You are not your face. Who you are is behind your face. You are who you are at heart.

The story is told of the woman preacher who was filled with the Holy Spirit and who would win for God the heart of the vilest sinner. But in society's eyes, she was ugly. One night during a campaign, a soldier on his way from work stopped at the meeting. All he could see during the sermon was the beauty of this preacher. So it was not surprising when he proposed to her and eventually married her. One day they decided to relax on the beach. The wife spread her mat out and lay on her back enjoying the feel of the sun on her body. Her husband looked at her and for the first time saw how ugly his wife was.

The Lord promised to beautify the meek with salvation. Her husband remembered this promise, then said to his wife, "Honey, get up and preach nuh!" For him, her beauty was seen only when she was under the anointing of the Holy Spirit.

Some of the most pleasant people are those who are classified as ugly. How astonishing it is at times to find out that those who are classified as beautiful are sometimes the most devious and selfish. That's not to say that you don't have pretty people who are beautiful on the inside too, but the point is that the body is simply the house for who you are; your inner being.

If you think of yourself as beautiful on the inside then you are beautiful; if you think of yourself as ugly on the inside then you are ugly. You will never be able to see yourself beyond your thoughts. For changes to take place in anyone, it has to start on the inside. The real you is inside. It is that spirit within you. That's why it is a private matter, one that only can be controlled by you. Hence, whatever change you want to make, it will have to be an individual endeavor and will require conscious effort.

When an individual decides to accept Christ as Lord of his or her life, it has to be done consciously. It's not done through magic. There has to be a reprogramming of the mind which will not happen overnight. It is a growth process. That's why it is important for such an individual to feed his or her mind on the word of God and to be in constant communication with Him. Philippians 4:8 says (KJV), "Finally, brethren, whatsoever things are true, whatsoever things are honest, whatsoever things are just, whatsoever things are pure, whatsoever things are lovely, whatsoever things are of good report, if there be any virtue, and if there be any praise, think on these things."

I conclude with a poem by Rumi:

You were born with potential
You were born with goodness and trust
You were born with ideals and dreams.
You were born with greatness.

You were born with wings.
You are not meant for crawling, so don't.
You have wings
Learn to use them and fly.

Give Yourself Away and Love It

One of the surest ways to put an inferiority complex in the dungeon where it belongs is to give yourself away and love it. The more you do this, the less time you will have to think of things that do not exist. But what do I mean when I say give yourself away? Do I mean allowing others to take advantage of you? Absolutely not. It simply means to get involved in meaningful activities that will be beneficial to you and to others. Let's look on some ways in which you can give yourself away:

- ***Get involved:***
- Every member in the church has a part to play no matter how simple. Get involved in the church school, the youth fellowship, the children's Bible club, to name a few. You can choose to serve as an usher or a missionary. Whatever area you think you are comfortable in, seek it. You don't have to start big; simple things like helping with the floral arrangement can help to boost your self-esteem and help you to feel appreciated and loved.
- Whatever you do, give it your best shot and take pride in it. Commit yourself to the task at hand, and I'm sure you will be awarded for it. I have no doubt that at the end of the day you will feel proud of yourself.
- Visit the hospital when you can and give a word of cheer to those who are less healthy than you at the moment. Just a simple smile and words such as *God be with you* can restore a sense of hope to the one in despair. Share a word of prayer with them and you

will find that by giving of yourself in this way you will add joy and worthwhileness to your life.

- If you want others to appreciate you, first you have to learn to appreciate them. Compliment those who should be complimented; tell someone how lovely he or she is; help an elderly person across the street and very soon you will attract the appreciation of others.
- Spend time with your family and let each member know how much you appreciate them. I remember my mother saying to my younger sisters, "Follow your sister's example." It made me feel good about myself knowing that my mom appreciated me for who I am. Practice saying *I love you.*
- Get involved in community activities. Don't just sit back and do nothing when there is something you can do to improve the lives of everyone around you. That was my motivation when I started the Bullock Heights Youth Club. I was glad that I could help young men and women find a sense of purpose for their lives. You don't have to start a youth club but there may be something else that you can do to help the growth and development of the community.
- Don't be afraid to share your opinion when the opportunity arises. It doesn't matter what others think of it, it's your opinion and is valuable to you, and maybe others will appreciate its value as well. However, at the same time, don't try to force it on others. Just state your mind and let it go. Be humble in whatever you do. Do not mistake humility for an inferiority complex. You can be verbose, but humble. Love whatever you do and soon you will not be the same. You will accept yourself, your self-esteem will improve, and then you'll be able to announce to the world that I AM PROUD TO BE ME. I'M GLAD I'M ME AND THAT'S MY CHOICE FROM NOW

> ON. I WILL TAKE CONTROL OF WHO I AM AS GOD HAS GIVEN ME THIS AUTHORITY.

I will end this chapter with the words of this song I love so much:

> Cause I'll rise again,
> Ain't no power on earth can keep me down,
> Cause I'll rise again,
> death can't keep me in the ground.

An inferiority complex will not keep you down for you have chosen to live above it. Nobody will be given control over how you feel about yourself. YOU ARE IN CONTROL!

Part Three

You Are God's

Chapter Eleven

God Believes In You

Ye have not chosen me but I have chosen you and ordained you that ye should go and bring forth fruits and that whatsoever ye shall ask in my name, He will do it you.

John 15:16

I was about nine years old when I told my mother, who at that time was the president of the Ladies Ministry at church, that I wanted to sing in the special Sunday night program. She responded, "Really? That would be great!" I then said to her that if I sang, I wanted to be paid. She was hysterical. I didn't know my mother had seriously considered my request until that same night in church I heard her telling the congregation humorously that I wanted to sing but would not unless I was paid.

I was called on to sing, so I did my favorite song, "I'm Bound for That City." I got a favorable response from the congregation and before I took my seat, my pastor, the late Pastor Waysome, gave me fifty cents! After that, I wanted to sing every night.

Often I have heard it said that encouragement sweetens labor, and what a blessing that fifty cents made in my life! From then on, I never stopped singing, though I don't get fifty cents any more. My pastor believed in me, just as God believes in you. But you may ask, "How can God believe in someone like me? Has He forgotten who I am? Doesn't He remember what I did ten years ago?" And then I hear Him say to you, "My dear child, I know you well. I know that you are sometimes stubborn and want to have your way, but I still believe in you. Let me remind you of my words in John 15:16. *Ye have not chosen me but I have chosen you, and ordained you, that ye should go and bring forth fruits, and that whatsoever ye shall ask in my name, He may give it you.* That's how much I believe in you."

"Oh God," you reply, "Thank you for believing in me. But God, what difference will it make to believe in me?"

"Oh my child, if you could only know. It will make a lot of difference, and if you believe in me, it will even get better. My child, you will never be the same again. The wretched person you thought yourself to be will experience a transformation that will send waves of electric shock to those who saw you as society's outcast. Your dignity and self-worth will be restored. I will declare you before all men. As Isaiah says, 'You shall be a crown of beauty in the hand of the Lord, and a royal diadem in the hand of your God'. (Isa. 62:3, ESV) That's what I will do for you. All men will respect you and others will want to emulate you. That's what John talks about in John 8:11 (ESV), 'neither do I condemn you. Go and sin no more'. Do you remember the woman who was caught in adultery? Everyone thought the worst of her, but I did not, as I believed in her, just as I believe in you. In addition, I will defend your dignity as I defended hers. Remember Luke 4:11 (NIV), 'they will lift you up in their hands, so that you will not strike your foot against a stone'. I will help to prevent you from going to pieces. You are a vessel that I cherish very much. I will be with you every step of the way, even when you think I have forgotten you. I will allow you to pick up the pieces and start all over again, because I believe in you."

God Knows You Well

When I was a child growing up, I would try to evade punishment for something I did wrong by covering up the truth of what really happened. But my mother could not be fooled, no matter how hard I tried. It is said that a mother always knows. And I somewhat agree. I know my children so well that I know what each is capable of, and I guess other mothers can say the same. And if we, who are carnal, can know our children so well, why wouldn't the God of all Gods, King of all Kings, our creator and friend, know us well? Psalm 100:3 says, "Know ye that the Lord is God, it is he that hath made us and not we ourselves. We are his children and the sheep of his pastures." And John 10:27 (KJV) says, "My sheep hear my voice, and I know them, and they follow me."

You can hide away from man, but not from God. He knows you well and, as a result, chose you to be who you are with great potential and ability. Hence, it makes no sense to sit idle, thinking that you *can't*, for God knows you *can*. As I have discussed before, He will never ask you to do anything that he knows you can't do. He knows your capability and incapability, your potentials and inadequacies, your strengths and weaknesses, likes and dislikes, and your joys and your sorrows. He will never give you too much or drive you into deep depression. You are there only because you failed to take him at his words; you have lost confidence, not because of any fault of his, but because you have allowed low-energy thoughts to dominate your conscious and subconscious mind.

He knows when you are in need and has given you the assurance that He will supply all your needs according to his riches in glory. Matthew 6:31-32 (KJV) says, "Therefore take no thought saying, What shall we eat? Or, What shall we drink? Or wherewithal shall we be clothed? . . . for your Heavenly Father knoweth that ye have need of all these things." He further assured you that just as He takes care of the sparrows and the flowers of the field, He will take care of you. If you could just learn to depend on your Creator as the rest of creation does, then you would not have half the problems you now have.

He knows the darts of the enemy and the areas of your life that he is planning to attack. But He will cloak you in his armor and not one of those darts will graze you. Conversely, however, He never promised that you will not experience storms in your life, but He will see you through them.

Nothing that happens in your life happens by chance. They are all for a reason. The devil can't put his hands on you if God does not give him the permission. He may allow you to think the worst of God as it is his nature to deceive you. Conquer him with all the spiritual resources at your disposal.

God knows you well and only uses your circumstances to strengthen your character, to restore your dignity, to develop faith in Him, and to increase the value of your self-worth. God knows when you've had enough. He knows when we have reached the brink. He is always on time and never late. He specializes in things thought impossible and will do for you what no other power can do.

Lazarus was dead for four days and Martha thought Jesus was late. As a matter of fact she said, "Lord, if you were here my brother would not die." But Jesus was not working off Martha's timetable. He saw and knew things that Martha did not know. He had the bigger picture in mind.

The following is a list of lessons the Lord wanted to teach us from Lazarus' death:

1. Jesus knows you well.
2. He can give back the life that was stolen from you.
3. He sets you free.
4. He has a bigger and better plan for you.
5. He will ask you to remove the hindrances and deal with the stench.
6. He wants to make you a living testimony.

So don't hurry God to work on your behalf. Wait on Him and be of good courage, for He knows you well.

Make a Difference for the God Who Believes in You

If God did not believe in you, He would not have entrusted you with His treasures. What treasures you may ask: your talents and abilities; your freedom of choice; a powerful mind; and the spirit within that speaks in a still, small voice. These are all treasures you were entrusted with. When, for example, you have used your talents and abilities for other purposes than glorifying God, or have used that powerful mind of yours to plot evil against your brothers and sisters, you are implanting hatred and wickedness in the universe.

Second to life, man was given the freedom of choice. But it has often been abused to the point where we want to deprive others—the demanding parents, the controlling husband, or the slave driver—of their right to this special gift. Evidence of this was first seen in the Garden of Eden. The devil manipulated Eve into eating of the forbidden fruit. She then seduced Adam to partake of it. They started to blame each other when they realized that they had done something wrong. But God held them accountable for the evil they had committed.

Freedom comes with responsibilities, and I have observed over the years that people do not know how to handle this. The more freedom they are given, the less responsible they become. When the Honorable P. J. Patterson, former Prime Minister of Jamaica, announced that his government would be paying for at least three CXC (Caribbean Examination Council) subjects, shouts of joy could be heard from his supporters in Sam Sharpe Square, Montego Bay, but especially from parents whose children were sure to sit the exams in the future. But I have noticed for a while that students take this opportunity for granted and do not study as hard as they would if the exam had been paid for by their parents. In addition, students who know they do not have the ability to sit these exams, insist on being signed up since the exams are paid for by the government and not by their parents.

All that God has blessed us with is intended for us to make a difference in our lives and in the lives of others. If we have a God who believes in us, wouldn't we want to make a difference for His sake?

One of the blessings of Jesus being the Lord of our lives is that He helps us to appropriately use these entrusted treasures. Let's look at love, for example. A popular song says, *It's love, it's love, it's love that makes the world go round.* When Jesus enters your life, He gives you the ability to love. If you say you love Christ and have no love for one another, then you are living a lie. God believes in you and expects you to make a difference in the way you treat others and His creation as a whole. All living things have a touch of God. All were given the gift of life. He created them all: the trees, the fish of the sea, animals, and man. All have to return from whence they came, which is why you need to be appreciative and make a difference in whatever you do.

Your talents and abilities were not given to you to be used selfishly, but rather to bring healing to those who are aching physically, emotionally, psychologically, spiritually. They were meant to enrich the lives of others. If you were blessed, for instance, with the ability to sing, then use it to educate and comfort others; if you were blessed with artistic ability, use it to enhance the lives of those who know how to appreciate such talent.

Your financial blessing was not given to be used as a weapon to manipulate others or to put you on a pedestal to be worshipped by those who are less fortunate. On the contrary, it was given so you can help improve the lifestyles of others, feed the hungry, and bring comfort to those who are dying from lack of medical attention. But how often do we turn a blind eye to those who are desperately seeking our attention: the poor and needy, the homeless, the suffering child, or the starving nation.

I have a problem today with churches that place more emphasis on having a beautiful edifice while there are many around—sometimes even in their congregation—who are longing for financial aid. Sometimes the very same are being pressured to contribute to the worthy cause. At some churches, if you do not want to feel embarrassed, you had better make sure you have something to put in that offering box. Don't get me wrong, I am not saying you should *not* give if God has blessed you; what I'm saying is that *giving* should be done freely from the heart, because doing it grudgingly will rob you of the blessing you should receive.

Many mothers and fathers seek comfort in harmful substances to escape the pain and suffering of not being able to afford to feed their children. Then they become abusive and controlling. They need help, and God will hold you accountable if you turn a blind eye to them.

You were promoted at work, not to bring honor to yourself, but to honor God in whatever you do. Many are depending on your valuable input to foster the growth of the company, which supplies bread to their families. Woe to you, if you use this blessing for your own selfishness and greed. I'm tired of reading in the papers of CEOs and others in high-paying positions who manipulate and rob others to acquire more wealth. Woe to the nurse who, because of neglect, caused the unnecessary suffering of those in his/her care.

You may have just joined the staff of an organization and realize that your colleagues spend more time gossiping with each other instead of administering drugs to the patients at the right time. You can make a difference. If you know that it is wrong, don't participate. You may be criticized, but as long as the criticism is a result of your doing your job well, don't worry for you will be blessed. Matthew 5:1-12 says, "Blessed are ye when men shall revile you, and persecute you, and shall say all manner of evil against you falsely, for my sake. Rejoice, and be exceedingly glad: for great is your reward in heaven: for so persecuted they the prophets which were before you." Likewise, woe to us teachers who deprive our students of a solid education by refusing to spend enough time in preparation and research. The life of our nation is in our hands. Education is the nourishment for a growing nation, so let's make a difference in the classroom.

In whatever field you are put to work, make it your aim to make a difference. Be joyful about what you do. Do it as to the Lord and not to men. Be enthusiastic about the difference you are about to make and watch God work in your life and bring you a reward you never expected to receive.

Chapter Twelve

Spiritual Intimacy

I am the vine, you are the branches. Those who remain in me and I in them, will produce much fruit. For apart from me, you can do nothing.

John 15:5, NLT

Spiritual intimacy is considered the fifth stage of intimacy in a marital relationship in which the individuals no longer see themselves as separate entities, but rather as one. At this stage, there is a sense of meaning to the relationship where certain morals, values, and ethics are shared. It is at this stage that the core of one being is connected to another. It is the time when one partner's joys and sorrows become the joys and sorrows of the other. It is the time when a partner's likes and dislikes are accepted and shared. It is the time of togetherness, a time of oneness.

Spiritual intimacy from a Biblical point of view, however, is the stage at which man becomes one with his Creator, with his God, with the Universal Intelligence. It is the time when man strives to be Christ-like rather than striving to be a Christian. It is the stage at which man gets connected to his source of origin. It is the time when the mind of Christ is implanted in man. It is no longer man, but the Christ that lives within man. It is the time when man recognizes Jesus as the true vine and he as the branch. At such time, man cannot survive apart from the vine, which is Jesus Christ. So man starts to think like Christ, speak like Christ, and act like Christ. It is at this stage where man can say like Christ, "I and my father are one." It is at this stage that man allows the spirit of God to rule in his heart, consequently defeating the dominance of his ego, which Dr. Wayne Dyer referred to as "edging God out." It is at this stage that man's character is built on the word of God, and he can now say, "It is not I that live, but the Christ who lives in me."

Man is in constant battle with self. There is a war between the spirit of good and the spirit of evil. It is the depth of man's relationship with God that will determine whether he succumbs or overcomes the evil influences around him.

The story is told of a grandfather who was talking to his grandson after the September 11, 2001 attack. He was heard telling the grandson that, "I have two wolves fighting inside of me. The first wolf is filled with anger, hatred, bitterness, and mostly revenge. The second wolf," he said, "is filled with love, kindness, compassion, and mostly forgiveness."

The little boy then inquired, "Which wolf do you think will win?"

The grandfather responded, "Whichever one I feed."

Spiritual intimacy is about feeding the wolf that portrays Christ-like attitudes. It should be the aim of every man to renew the fellowship that he once had with God in the Garden of Eden, where God would come down in the cool of the day to have a regular rap session with man.

Develop a Relationship with God

One of the beauties in life is to find a partner with whom you are compatible, one with whom you can share, who will be a friend, and somebody who will be with you through good times and bad times. Somebody who will accept you for who you are no matter the many faults you have and who will see the good you can become, rather than the bad that you are. One such partner is the God who made you a little higher than the angels in heaven.

The first step in developing this kind of relationship is to make Christ the master of your life. You do so by asking him to forgive you of your sins and, in return, accept his forgiveness by faith. The Apostle Paul said in Romans 3:23, "For all have sinned and come short of the glory of God." But Christ is willing to forgive you of your sins no matter how messed up you are. "Though your sins be as scarlet, they shall be as white as snow." (Isa 1:18)

If Christ is the master of your life, you will have to focus your thoughts on Him every day. Remember I discussed in an earlier chapter that you are your thoughts? Daily prayer and Bible reading are essential for the mind of Christ to be in you. You cannot maintain or develop a relationship with God without these two. They are the required nutrients to maintain a positive and healthy spiritual lifestyle. Bible reading is God talking directly to you; prayer is your talking directly to God. You may ask, "Does God only speak to me through his words?" The answer is "No." There are other means of communication: nature, our circumstances, our inner being, or through other people.

Before I came to the United States of America, everything began to go haywire. My mortgage was in arrears, and I could not clear it up being in Jamaica (or so I thought). I was hardly getting anything in my paycheck. I could not get another loan from the bank, as I was in the process of paying back loans I had borrowed already. All doors were closed in my face, except one: to go to the United States. I spoke to God about my situation, and His answer was to come to the United States. As a result, I never hesitated. I had my children transferred to other schools in Mandeville before I left. So this is one way that God speaks through our circumstances.

When you have an intimate relationship with God, you will be able to recognize His voice when He speaks. Too many times

God speaks to us and we pay no attention to what He is saying, as we are either too busy or are unable to recognize His still, small voice. If in your heart you feel that you should do something after you have prayed about it, go for it. At times though, it is good to be quiet about it and watch God work. Many times when we share to the wrong people what we think God is saying to us we become discouraged. Listen to the still, small voice within you and move accordingly. *If God be for you, then who can be against you?*

Why is it necessary to develop a relationship with God? Since he is your creator and designer and has put you here on earth to accomplish His purpose, He knows you very well. He wants you to be partners with Him. You are His agent. Of God's creation, man is given the ability to reason and to think things through. God knows your future and is the best one to guide you through it. He has all the tools and equipment that you will need to live a successful and prosperous life. You can only know your true purpose when you have a relationship with God. Since He is the architect of your life, who would know you better?

Just like with any other friendship, friendship with God must be maintained. I lost true friends because of non-communication. Keep in touch with God no matter where you are or the time of day. He is never too busy for you. He is always on the line. Talk with Him, laugh with Him, and celebrate with Him. He can be your all-in-all, your counselor. If there is a decision you have to make, He can help you to make it. I have a friend who consulted God about a simple matter as perming her hair! The point is God is interested in even the simple matters of life.

He will be your provider. How many times are we unable to see our way through a particular situation and then God just opens doors and windows that we never thought possible? Have we forgotten that God specializes in things thought impossible? Sometimes it is at the point when we feel like giving up that God comes through for us.

Remember the disciples were toiling all night and never caught a fish? Then Jesus came along and instructed them to cast their nets out into the deep. As with anyone with experience, they began to argue that it was useless, but since Jesus instructed them they did it anyway and what a catch it was! Their nets were broken. That's the God I am talking about.

He is not only our counselor and provider, but also our healer. The pessimist thinks that God's healing power was only in Bible days, but the fact is God is the same yesterday, today, and forevermore. He never changes. This gives us the assurance that we can be healed of our infirmities even when the doctors say otherwise.

We are made to believe that the doctor can do more for us than God. We fail to appreciate the fact that it is actually God who works through them to do what they do. If God does not want you healed, then no matter the doctor's expertise, it will never happen. So instead of giving the credit to the doctor, give it to God. He is the wonder worker. Claim your healing in Jesus' name.

I felt a tremor in my leg when it was in a relaxed state. All kinds of negative thoughts began to go through my head. *Yes, Maizie, you are going to have a nervous breakdown; yes, Maizie, yes, the doctors were right, you are coming down with Parkinson's disease.* But each time I felt it, I said to God, "God, you are my healer and if you can't stop this tremor then no doctor can. You created me and know how every single organ in my body should work and for that reason, I trust you for my healing." With time, it went away. I kept the affirmation that this problem is not too big for God to fix. Sometimes our healing does not come immediately; it comes in stages over a period of time, especially if it is psychological.

God also will be your source of strength. When the going gets tough and the tough get going, He will be there to take you through. When I was going through a rough period in my life, God assured me of his constant presence. This was done through

Isaiah 41:10-12, which says, "Fear not Maizie [I inserted my name] for I am with you. Be not dismayed for I am thy God. I will strengthen thee; yea I will help thee; yea I will uphold thee with the right hand of my righteousness. Behold all they that are incensed against thee shall be ashamed and confounded; they shall be as nothing and they that strife with thee shall perish." What consolation! Has He disappointed me? No. He came through for me at the time, and He will do the same for you. Just trust Him.

In 2 Corinthians 12:9 Paul said, "And he said unto me, 'My grace is sufficient for thee: for my strength is made perfect in my weakness'." He will direct your steps. God, the Universal Intelligence, knows what is best for you and can tell you if the decision you are about to make is the right one. He will never lead you in the path of destruction. He loves you too much. He celebrates when you trust Him to lead the way for you.

At this moment, while I am writing, I want to return to Jamaica after spending five years in the United States. Some people say, "No, don't go. I don't think you are making the right decision." But I am going to listen to God and do according to His instructions. If He wants me to stay, then I will stay. If He wants me to go, then I will go. Wherever He leads, I will follow. He is the best navigator. Yes, the path He leads may be rocky and full of potholes, but I have confidence that it will be all right.

Cultivate an intimate relationship with God and anticipate the rich blessings He will bestow upon you, your spouse, your children, and your family in general. This is a relationship in which you will never lose.

Representing Christ to the World

God must be very aggrieved about the way we represent Him to the world sometimes as a mean, unforgiving, and cruel God; a God who is only for Himself and does not have interest in others; an uncaring and mean-spirited God; a God who is only present on Saturdays or Sundays; a God who loves to make promises He can't keep; an unjust God who cares only for the rich and not for the poor; or a God who is only interested in those who are interested in Him. Some of us who are called Christians should be ashamed of our poor representation of Christ to the world. No wonder people's hearts become hardened and think that choosing the path of Christ is a waste of time. You are called to represent Christ to the world. You were specially chosen and were placed in your small corner to "let your light so shine before men that they may see your good work and glorify your father in heaven." (Matt. 5:16) A life without Christ is a life in darkness, but a little light will dispel all darkness. "A candle set on a candlestick will give light unto all that are in the house."

Jesus Christ is depending on you to give hope to those in despair; to bring joy to those who are unhappy; to destroy the seeds of evil and cultivate the land with good seeds; to encourage the spirit of forgiveness where there is bitterness.

It grieves my spirit when I hear people God has chosen to represent him to the world say things like, "As long as I live, I will never speak to him/her again!" Or, "It serves him/her right. It should have happened before. Let him/her be destroyed." If you have Christ within, then these thoughts will not take root in your heart to the point where you become cynical, envious, and unforgiving. Where Christ is, there is love and forgiveness. Bitterness, malicious thoughts, envy, deceitfulness, unforgivable acts, selfishness and pride, arrogance and deception can't grow on Christ-like soil. If we say we love God and then hate our brother, the truth is not in us.

As a Christian, Christ should be seen in every area of your life: in your speech, your attitude towards others, your work, and any other responsibilities you may have. In other words, your entire life should be affected. As a child of God, you should not go around with the weight of the world upon your shoulders, for God promised to be your burden bearer. He said in 1 Peter 5:7,

"Casting all your care upon him for He careth for you." Matthew 11:29 says, "Take my yoke upon you and learn of me for I am meek and lowly in heart; and ye shall find rest."

When you walk around with guilt dominating your life, you are representing Christ as an unforgiving God! He left all the splendor of His good life in heaven and came into this sinful world to pay the price for your sins. Yet, if you refuse to accept His forgiveness, watch your life become unproductive and acquire the state of bitterness. Isaiah 64:6 tells us, "But we are all an unclean thing, and all our righteousness are as filthy rags, and we all do fade as leaf; and our iniquities, like wind, have taken us away." So arise from your state of guilt and move on with your life. That's what Christ expects you to do.

The prodigal son lived for a long time in guilt and shame, eating the pigs' food, but he never sat thinking he would not be forgiven by his father. He never continued to waddle in guilt and shame; instead, he said, "I will arise and go to my father." And did his father reject him? No! As a matter of fact his father was always at the gate looking out for him. He anticipated the day when his son would return. Similarly, God is looking out for you when you return with your guilt and shame.

Poverty and sickness seem to be on the increase in our society. Children are dying from starvation; people are hungry. It is time we do what little we can to eradicate as much as possible the plagues that are robbing us of our joy and happiness. It is very disturbing to see children suffering, especially in parts of Africa.

When Jesus was on earth, He was always doing well. He fed the multitude, restored sight to the blind, improved the health of people, and brought back life to the dead. His heart always went out with love and compassion to the needy, especially to children. As a matter of fact, He said, "Suffer the little children to come unto me and forbid them not for such is of the Kingdom of heaven." If we are His representatives, He expects us to do likewise and be sensitive to the needs of others.

"Put on the whole armor of God that you may be able to withstand the wiles of the devil." (Eph. 6:11) That's the only sure way to do what Christ requires of you. Give a smile to somebody, as you might just save that person from thinking the world is against him or her.

Remember, you can only be a true representative if you stay connected to your source, Jesus Christ. He alone can give you the strength and wisdom needed to epitomize Him to the world.

God's Words—The Spiritual Navigator to True Success

Sometimes we are misled into thinking that true success is found in our external achievements: houses, lands, expensive cars, education, and the like. But true success is not measured by these, but rather by how we view ourselves, what we have achieved, and where we are in light of God's words and His purpose for our lives.

The man who cheats and steals to obtain what he wants will never experience true success as his conscience—the cry of his heart, mind, and soul—will bring about such discomfort that he will never experience joy, love, peace, and contentment. Consequently, he will bury himself in drugs, alcohol, or sex, as a means to disguise his pain.

God's word is the navigator to true success. It will bring you rich rewards both internally and externally. Joshua, the son of Nun, after the death of Moses, was commanded to follow God's instructions, as this was a sure guarantee to being successful. Likewise, if you follow the word of God you will be like a "tree planted by the rivers of water that bringeth forth fruits in due season. Your leaves also shall not wither and whatsoever you doeth shall prosper."

David says in Psalms 119:105, "Thy word is a lamp unto my feet and a light unto my path." He said further in Psalms 119:11,

"Thy word have I hid in my heart that I might not sin against thee."

Drivers today depend heavily on the navigator to move them from point A to point B. It has become such a necessity, especially for those whose jobs involve a lot of travelling. It is a helpful device, but only if the right information is programmed into it. I have known of instances where drivers arrived at an unintended destination as a result of wrong input. This was the case with a friend who was coming to visit me for the first time. What should have taken him half an hour took him an hour!

The word of God will help you find your true self. You will discover your true potential and ability and maintain your equilibrium of joy, peace, love, and contentment. On the contrary, if you are experiencing an inward imbalance, you will also experience an outward imbalance. The way we perceive the world is a result of our internal state. If you are not inwardly joyful, you will never be externally joyful. And that is why, to a certain extent, you have the power to change your view of the world. You have the power to attract true success. If presently you are struggling with quilt, shame, anger, sadness, frustration, embarrassment, or hurt, you will never be able to experience the flow of God's blessings in your life. These negative emotions will have to be handed to him for you to have joy, peace, love, and contentment in your life simply by trusting God's promises.

True success requires our involvement. Too many times we sit down and expect God to bless us when we are doing nothing to help ourselves. You cannot be passive. You will have to do what you can and let God do what you can't do for yourself. It is like driving a car. You will never get this car to go where you want it to go unless you turn the ignition and do the steering. The rest is up to the engine. If it's a workable engine then it should start moving.

I was inspired to write this book, but if I had sat down and done nothing, you would not be reading it right now. You need to move from the state of being a quitter or a camper to that of a climber. When the pressure of the journey reaches you and you feel like giving up, rely on the word of God to pull you to the top of the mountain. His word says, "I can do all things through Christ which strengtheneth me."

God's promises are given to reassure us of his love and interest in our daily lives. The day before I wrote this chapter, I came upon his promise in Isaiah 43:1–4 (NLT), which says,

> Do not be afraid, for I have ransomed you. I have called you by name, you are mine. When you go through deep waters, I will be with you. When you go through rivers of difficulties, you will not drown. When you walk through the fire of oppression, you will not be burned up, the flames will not consume you. For I am the Lord, your God, the holy One of Israel, your Savior. . . . I traded their lives for yours because you are precious to me. You are honored, and I love you.

Isn't this a wonderful assurance? How can we not experience true success when we adhere to the word of God? There is no way the defeating blocks of fear, anxiety, procrastination, indecision, depression, blame, indifference, judgment, perfectionism, self-pity, confusion, or guilt, can hinder us from achieving success, not just success, but TRUE success if we adhere to the word of God.

No matter the problem you are faced with, God's word has the power to help you overcome them. And you know what? His words will never return unto Him void. The mission must be accomplished. If you believe and act upon them, there is no way that you will be the same.

Whenever I have a decision to make and am struggling with indecision, I remember His promise in Joshua 1:7, "Only be thou strong and very courageous, that thou mayest observe to do according to all the laws, which Moses thy servant commanded thee. Turn not from it to the right or to the left, that though mayest prosper whithersoever though goest." I will read this over and over again, especially the last phrase. I will insert my name into it so that it speaks to me directly. As long as I know that my decision is in accordance to God's word then I know that He will be with me no matter the outcome.

When God told Abraham to offer Isaac, the son of his old age and one he loved dearly, Abraham, though he may have experienced sadness, never disobeyed God. He knew that once God gave an instruction it was to be for his good. So even though it may be painful, if God says do it, then do it. In the end Abraham was blessed with a lamb for the sacrifice.

If you are in an abusive relationship and you hear the voice of God telling you to leave, do not go on wondering how you are going to survive, for God has already made the provision. Just leave. God will not close a door without opening another. Rise up and take control of your life for God is there to help you.

Many times God speaks to us and we refuse to listen because what he is saying is not what we want to hear. But if we want to have true success, we have to listen or else we may get what we want but end up regretting it. Listen attentively as you read the word of God. Just as the instructor in your navigation system tells you the turns that you should make, so is it with the Holy Spirit. He is the instructor through the word of God. Allow Him to be your guide and experience the transformation of your internal world as it attracts success in your outer world.

Chapter Thirteen

In Everything Give Thanks

Giving thanks always for all things unto God and the father of our Lord Jesus Christ.

Ephesians 5:20

Man has an insatiable appetite and desire. He is never satisfied. Of all creations, man is the most dissatisfied, and as a result is always complaining. He complains there is too much rain; he complains there is too much sunshine; he complains when he is full; he complains when he is empty; he complains when he is going through difficult times; he complains when things are going well. He is always complaining.

The flowers and the trees, the birds and the fishes, the animals and beasts of the field play their role in the universe without complaint. The ants do not say, "Why did God allow winter?" Instead they accept the fact that there won't always be spring, autumn, or summer, and there is winter. As a result, instead of complaining, they prepare their homes for the winter and have it stocked with enough food.

If man could cooperate with the natural principles of the universe, then this world would be a better place. If man could substitute the urge to complain with that of thanksgiving, then he would live a fulfilled and satisfying life and no doubt relieve himself of unnecessary pain and the agony of a dissatisfied and ungrateful heart.

The children of Israel spent many years suffering as slaves in Egypt. They prayed and cried for God to bring them deliverance from the cruel hands of Pharaoh and his people. For forty years, God prepared Moses for the task of bringing these people freedom, and, at last, they were freed. But when they came upon their first obstacle—the Red Sea—their thankfulness and praise were compromised by complaints and regrets. At one point they wished they were still in Egypt. But are we better than they? No! Until we have learned to be thankful to God for the situations we face in life, will we start to experience the blessings of the Lord.

A friend of mine had a stroke in his bathtub one morning as he was hurrying to start his planned day. He was discovered about two hours after the attack, and he was grateful to God for having spared his life. As time went by and he thought there should be more signs of improvement in his ability to walk, he began to complain. Thanks go to his wife, however, who was there to remind him of how blessed he had been. He may not have been walking like he used to, but thanks to God he was walking!

Ephesians 5:20 reminds us to be thankful always. It says, "Giving thanks always for all things unto God and the father of our Lord Jesus Christ." It is important to note that it says always, not only when things are going well, but always. Not only in good health, but also in bad health; not only for our fine accomplishments, but also when things are not going the way you want them to. When the mountain seems hard to climb, give thanks you are at the foot of it and not below it. That's a sign that you are alive and, where there is life, there is hope. It is hoped that at the end of this chapter you will develop the habit of giving thanks through all circumstances in life.

In the Midst of the Storm

One Sunday in June, 1988, we got the bad news that our mother had been diagnosed with cervical cancer. We were devastated.

The tears streamed down the faces of all those who loved and appreciated her. As the oldest child, I really did not know what to do. I thought, *What if my mother should die, what will happen to us?* I was the only one out of school; all of my siblings were in high school. The pain of loneliness and of an uncertain future gripped my heart.

I had never seen my father cry so much. At that moment he was probably thinking that this was too much for anyone to bear. My mother was only forty-five years old and in the prime of her life! This really was a storm we were going through. My father, at that time, had never had a stable job. As a matter of fact, I was the only one with such. But how could I take care of my mother with a meager salary? In the midst of the storm we were assured that God would take care of all our needs, so there was no need to worry. Family members and friends assisted in ways that were unbelievable.

During my mother's period of illness, Romans 8:28 became my consolation. "For we know that all things work together for good to them that love the Lord, and are called according to his purpose." God came through for us and on August 17, 1988, about three months after Mother was diagnosed, God called her home. Though I miss her I am glad she went home to be with the Lord. The pain was more than she could bear.

God did not promise us sunshine only, but some rain and some very stormy nights. He gave us the assurance that He will never leave us, nor forsake us, that He will be with us always, even to the end of the world. For this we can say, "Thank you, Lord."

Great multitudes followed Jesus everywhere he went. After one such occasion, He told his disciples to cross to the other side of the lake. They started out and as soon as they began to sail across, Jesus settled down for a nap. Very soon afterwards, a fierce storm arose and the boat began to sink and fill with water. Hypnotized by fear, the disciples woke up Jesus shouting, "Master, Master, we are going to drown!"

When Jesus woke up, he rebuked the wind and the raging sea and suddenly the storm stopped. Then all was calm. He asked them, as he is asking you today, "Where is your faith?" The scripture says the disciples were terrified and amazed, that they asked each other, "What manner of man is this that the wind and the waves obeyed his voice?"

You may be going through the storm of losing a loved one, but Jesus will see you through. There is no storm that He cannot calm. He will be your guide all the way and will bring you comfort and joy. He will fill the void that you may now be experiencing. And later on you will look back and say, "How did I do it?"

I know a gentleman who came to live in our community with his wife and two children. They were a prospering family; one that the community held with great regard. His daughter, the younger of the two children, was granted a government scholarship because of her great performance in the Common Entrance Examination, but unfortunately, she never lived to enjoy the opportunity. She died before starting high school.

Very soon afterwards, the son, who was an excellent achiever in high school, drowned in a tank at the school. And as if his storm was not strong enough, his wife died very shortly after.

This man had it all. Enough was enough, but in the midst of the storm, God was there with him and He not only calmed the storm, but also gave the man the wisdom and courage to fight other storms that will appear in his life.

You see, my friend, you are chosen for your storm, and you have been given all that is needed to keep your boat afloat no matter how rough the sea may be. The storm may rage high, but don't give up; keep holding on. After the storm, there is calm, and the truth is that no storm lasts forever; they are just for a time; they are temporary.

I remember Hurricane Gilbert in 1988, exactly one month after my mother died. The younger generation who has never experienced a storm was really looking forward to it. Little did we know how devastating it would be. People who did not have a relationship with God began to call on him to protect them. Trees were rooted up; homes were destroyed; lives were lost. Our roof left its place of comfort to a place we have not yet discovered. If my mother had been alive at that time, I don't think she would have survived it. I'm sure her pain would have been intensified.

You may be wondering why God allows you to go through storms. You may never know the answer, but you can be assured that it happened for a reason and a very good one, too. Simply say to yourself *this too shall pass*.

I have been through a lot of storms in my life: the loss of my mother, the loss of my home, the separation of my family, the loss of my baby. But these storms have made me stronger and wiser. I am prepared to face any other storm that may appear in my life, for I know in whom I believe, and I am persuaded that He is able to see me through.

Don't fall into the trap of self-pity. Don't allow guilt to destroy you. Don't ask, "Why me, Lord?" Instead, hold to your anchor which is Jesus Christ. Don't lose faith. Keep on trusting, keep believing, dispel all doubts and fears from your mind, and rest on the faithful promises of God. Say to your sickness, "Sickness, in the name of Jesus, you will never get me down. In God I put my trust and the gates of hell shall never prevail. The doctors may say there is no hope, but they don't have the final say. God does. He promised to restore health to my body and that I believe. No matter how long it takes, I will wait until my change comes."

Rebuke the demons of abuse from your family. Believe God will come through for you. Trust him to bring justice to the abuser and for him to change his ways. Don't allow fear to cause you to live in denial. Come forward and speak against it. The Lord promised to be your guide. Psalm 23:1 says, "Yea, though I walk through the valley of the shadow of death I will fear no evil for thou art with me, thy rod and thy staff they comfort me."

It may sound ironic to be thankful for your storms, but that is what the Lord requires of you. He wants you to thank Him for who He is: your Savior from all the storms in your life. You were only brought through them because God knew that you could bear them and after the experience, you would be a better person.

The song *One More Valley* says:

Don't let Satan see your fears,
Try to smile through your tears,
Hold your head up high and give the world a smile.
You must be faithful all the way,
It will be worth it all someday,
For your trials had only come to make you strong.

Remember in everything give thanks, even for your storms, as in the midst of the storm, the Lord will come to your rescue. Continue to trust His power to bring calmness to the winds and waves in your life.

When God Is Nowhere to be Found

I anxiously awaited the response of a friend who promised us that we would have an apartment for the first of December. I really wanted to get away because my baby was due in the next six months and living at the present apartment was a nightmare.

It was the last Saturday of the month. I got up and could not find the energy to do anything in the apartment. I should have been getting the response, and was disappointed when I was told that the house would not be available. With tears streaming down my face, I felt as though God had deserted me; that he was nowhere to be found. I cried, "Lord, what have I done to you? Why have you forsaken me?"

About half an hour later, I felt the urge to leave the house. I got my daughter, Monique, and dressed her, and we went to my cousin's home. As we entered her door, she said to me, "Maizie, I heard of an apartment for rent." We never hesitated. When we got to the place, the landlord, as I assumed her to be at the time, said to me, "You've come for the apartment."

A bit surprised, I asked her, "How did you know that?" Her response was that for some reason her spirit told her so. Without any further discussion, she handed me the keys and told me it was mine if I liked it and of course I did. God came through for me.

When it seems as though God is nowhere to be found and that you are walking this journey alone, remember He is there with you. He is only a little step ahead of you, preparing the path, installing light bulbs in the areas that would be too dark for you to see.

Our children sometimes do not think that we know the best for them and so it is with us. We sometimes don't understand God's ways. Jesus said to Mary and Martha, "You do not understand what I am doing but later you will." God does not expect us to understand, but rather to trust him and to wait patiently on him until our change comes.

For everything that goes wrong in your life there are lessons to be learned, even if it is just a reminder of who God is. When you are in the battle no harm will befall you as "He will give his angels charge over thee." You may call on him with no response, but he is closer than you can ever think or imagine and he has everything under control.

During moments when God seems far away, I sing songs of consolation. One of my favorites is:

> I care not today what the morrow may bring, if shadow or sunshine or rain. The Lord I know he ruleth over everything and all of my worry is vain.

A song in times of sorrow brings hope and peace and a tranquility that reminds me to stand still and let God have his way.

On Labor Day 2008 in the United States, I decided not to go to Brooklyn. I chose to stay home and fast about problems that I was experiencing at that time in my life. I prayed and focused on the latter part of Joseph's life in Egypt, and indeed I was blessed. Just at the time when I was about to break the fast, my phone rang, and my father was on the other line. He brought me the shocking news that my husband had taken the children without discussing the matter with me.

During that moment, I felt as though the weight of the world was on my shoulders. I then said to father, "Papa, I know that you are a praying father and I know that my step-mother is a praying mother. So I'm presently on my knees. I want you to join with me in prayer."

After praying, I got off my knees and took up my Bible and opened it to Psalm 46. Verse 10 got my attention. It said, "Be still and know that I am God. I will be exalted among the heathen; I will be exalted in the earth." At that moment, the anger that I felt subsided and was replaced with a peace that only God could give. In the end, it worked out for the good.

So, my friends, when it seems God is nowhere to be found, trust Him nevertheless. He is with you and will be with you every step of the way. He said in Isaiah 45:3, "I will give you the treasures of darkness, riches stored in secret places, so that you may know that I am the Lord who calls [you] by name." It is in the moment when God can't be felt, that He shares things, which strengthen you.

Why Should You Give Thanks

It is easy for us to give thanks when things are going our way, but when we are faced with problems, we have the tendency to cast blame, to complain, to murmur, and to forget that God is in control. You may ask, "Why should I give thanks when my business is not growing? Why should I give Him thanks when my health is failing? Why should I give Him thanks when my children are not doing well in school? Or why should I thank Him when it seems He has forgotten that I exist?"

Here are two reasons why God should be thanked no matter what your experience is.

1. ***For he alone is God.*** He is the creator of the universe and has an infinite wisdom. Man's wisdom cannot be compared to that of God. He is referred to by Dr. Wayne Dyer as the Universal Intelligence. Isaiah 47:8-11 says, "Do not forget this, keep it in mind. Remember this you guilty one. For I alone am God." God knows the knowhow, He knows why you are going through the pain you are experiencing right now. He knows where you are right now. He knows why you are having financial difficulties; He knows why you can't get pregnant no matter how hard you've tried. He knows all things and understands your pain more than you think He does.
2. ***For he is faithful and just.*** God's words will not return unto Him void. Whatever He promised in his words that will He do. Even when things seem not to be working out, God is behind the scene working them out for you. So don't become discouraged when it feels like you are all alone and God is not hearing you. He expects you to trust Him no matter what. Learn to pray about it and leave it in God's hands and do not go back to retrieve it. When I was younger and received gifts from my friends, I used them immediately so as to prevent my friends from retrieving them. Similarly, we are quick to take back from the Lord what we give Him, as though it's too hard for Him to carry. The scripture says, "Casting all your cares upon him; for He careth for you." 1 Peter 5:7 (KJV)

Chapter Fourteen

Don't Blame Another . . . It's Your Lack

The prudent person foresees danger and takes precaution. The simpleton goes blindly and suffers the consequences.

Proverbs 22:3

One evening at home while living in the United States, I got a call from my sister who suffers from epilepsy. She is hoping to be well again and has often declared healing. But on this particular day, she was not telling me of God's healing power upon her life, but rather that she thought that her nerves were playing all kinds of tricks on her.

After listening to her I said, "Don't blame what is happening in your life on your sickness. It is your lack: your lack in believing in the healing power of God; your lack in defeating the enemy's plan to use your sickness as a means of dictating the course of your life." How many times have we blamed our sicknesses, our environment, our dysfunctional families, our teachers, our spouses, or our broken relationships for our lack? It is time we stop blaming others and take the blame unto ourselves as a result of our lack. I have a friend who will never take responsibility for his actions. There is always someone or something to be blamed.

In the Garden of Eden, Adam blamed Eve. He said to God, "The woman whom thou gavest to be with me, she gave me of the tree, and I did eat." Genesis 3:12 (KJV) Eve, on the other hand, blamed the serpent. I wish I knew who the serpent blamed! He probably would have blamed God for creating him.

It is the general tendency for us to blame others when things go wrong in our lives. Nobody wants to be held accountable. It takes a person with genuine character and integrity to say, "I'm sorry. It is my fault." If this attitude were displayed in marriage relationships, maybe the divorce rate would not have escalated so rapidly. Today it appears as though nobody stays married. I salute those couples who are married for forty years or more. When I asked a former boss what had kept him and his wife together for over fifty years his response was, "Love and respect for each other." We, the younger generation, need to take a page out of our elders' book.

Change will never come to anyone unless an evaluation is done of one's self and there is a desire for the change. You have to be able to analyze the behavior and recognize the need for change. And as with any other thing, change is not easy. It comes with pain. If you stop blaming your inadequacies and unproductive life on sicknesses, financial disabilities, labels you have received in the past, your inheritance, or even others interfering in your life, you will receive the wisdom and courage to lead the life God intended you to have.

If a former supervisor of mine had blamed his inability to walk on another, he would not be spreading the Gospel from his wheelchair. He has the courage to accept what he cannot change and finds other avenues to make his life productive.

Whatever state you may be in today, don't allow self-pity to captivate you and bring you lower than God intended you to be. Look carefully at your life and take responsibility, for God has given you the ability to steer your own life.

In Jamaica, it is common to say *A nuh so so so* if your life did not go the way others thought it should have gone. In other words, somebody is preventing you from being what you should be. But I have come to realize that no one can stand in your path of progress except you and your negative beliefs. Don't forget that you are your thoughts, and if you continue to think that you can't make it, then you will never make it.

May this chapter give you the wisdom, courage, and strength to rise above your circumstances to be the person that God intended you to be. If you don't, it is your LACK!

Failed Success . . . It's Your Lack

Religious leaders who inflict guilt upon their members by allowing them to believe that the only success God desires is spiritual success are speaking contrary to the word of God. These preachers are afraid to preach financial prosperity. Some only do it when it concerns building a beautiful edifice or taking care of their personal needs. They call it *sow a seed.* As a result, members relax into a mediocre lifestyle and think it is not godly to be prosperous. They embrace a lack of self-confidence and call it humility. They refuse to go after their God-given dreams; dreams that God intended for them to use to enhance His creation.

It is true that not all men were created to be rich, but *to whom much is given, much is expected.* So it is wrong for you to sit down on your talents and abilities instead of making yourself useful to God. It is not a lack of opportunity, but your lack in seizing the opportunity. It is not a lack of finance, but a lack of your ability to plan your finances. It is not a lack of medical attention, it is your lack of faith. It is not the disobedience of your children, it is your lack of good parental guidance.

Being away from my children has taught me a lot about my lack. Looking back on the reasons for migrating to the United States, I realize that maybe if I had exercised a little more faith I would not have spent time away from them. Hence, it is not my lack of financial opportunities; it is my lack of faith. I have learned, however, not to cry over spilt milk. The past is the past and should be used to propel us forward into a brighter future.

Let's stop feeling sorry for ourselves and the wrong decisions that we sometimes make. Let us sit down with conscious effort and eradicate our lack. I hope that we will not sit down and cry over our lack like my younger daughter who called me crying that her daddy had killed a rat. Even though it was a rodent that destroys anything in its path, Annakay still thought that its life should have been preserved. No wonder she dreams of being a veterinarian.

You don't have to succumb to your lack, no matter what it is. In Christ, there is no lack. Through Christ you can be all that you ever want to be. He will give you far more than you ever thought or imagined. There is nothing too good that God won't give you as long as you are prepared to receive it. And again, you must be thankful for all things. Your worst days could be a period of preparation for the good things God has in store for you.

While working as a caregiver in the United States, I often think I am wasting my time. But each time I open my mouth to complain, that quiet voice says to me, "Shhhh, Maizie, you are here for a purpose. You are on training ground. I provided time for you to write your book (not that you are cheating on your employer's time, rather that you have made use of the available time). If you only knew what I have in store for you, then you would relax and make use of what you have."

The universe contains all that you will ever need to enhance your life and have a little heaven on earth. For you to receive the goodies, you have to be determined, and, with the help of God, get rid of your lack.

Daniel proposed in his heart that he would do nothing to dishonor God. As a result, he was thrown into a den of lions for praying to God three times a day. But he knew the God he served; a God who would be able to deliver him from being devoured. He trusted God. He could have become fearful—who wouldn't have? But he never allowed fear to create a lack; he maintained his faith in God and God came through for him.

As I relate Daniel's story, a thought comes that he could not destroy his lack without a conscious effort. First, I think he acknowledged his lack, and then he made a conscious effort to eliminate the lack by relying on the strength and power of the Lord. And that is exactly what you need to do. Here I will reemphasize the steps to defeat your lack:

1. Look where you are and acknowledge your lack. You may have been sitting down on your dream for years. Take a good look at yourself and ask the question, "Why am I not doing what I want to do? Is it a lack of self-confidence, a lack of faith, a lack of perseverance, or is it a lack of finance?"
2. Write down the ways in which you plan to defeat your lack. Are you going to trust God to fulfill his promise in your life? Are you going to get up from where you are and stop putting things off for a next time? Are you going to prepare a budget to see how you need to finance your project?
3. For each small step you've taken, give the honor and glory to God for helping you. Remember, you don't have to start with big steps, you just have to start with small ones. Make a list of these small steps (you may need to reread chapter four). One thing I know for sure is that each step you take will bring you closer to the fulfillment of that which you hope to achieve.
4. Keep your focus. Don't look at how fast your friend is moving. You do not all go at the same speed. The race is not for the swift, but for they who have endured to the end. When I walk with my girlfriend, Marcia, I have to make two stride to her every one to keep up with her. It reminds me of a poem I learned in third grade.

When Daddy walks with Jean and me,
We have a lot of fun,
For we can't walk as fast as he,
Unless we skip and run.

I stretched and stretched my legs so far,
I nearly slip and fall,
But how does Daddy walk so fast,
He doesn't stretch at all.

Another point I'd like to share is to make sure you use the right weapons to conquer your lack, or else you will be fighting a losing battle. Don't use envy, malice, strife, stealing, or arrogance to eradicate your lack, as with time it will resurface, and you will find yourself right back where you started. Or you may just reach where you want to go, but find out that you have nothing to maintain the height. A strong foundation is required to overcome your lack.

As a teenager, I envied anyone who could climb a tree, especially my sisters who had no problem climbing. As a result, I thought I would try to climb a small apple tree close to the house. I did it when no one was around, as I was afraid I would be laughed at. I pushed myself up and hung onto the lower branches. With that support, I went up in the tree. I remember saying to myself how proud I was. But then, forgetting that I was acrophobic, I looked down and became panic-stricken. Tears began to roll profusely down my face. Since there was no one to assist me, I grabbed hold of my fear, and with great care and effort, I climbed from the tree. From that day, I never climbed a tree again!

Go after what you want after you are sure that is what you want. The universe will provide you with all that you want to achieve your goal. Commit your lack to the God who can lock all lacks and work through you to bring about the best in you. Again don't blame another, it is your lack.

Dominate Sickness—It Is Your Lack

Time after time we hear of cases where doctors tell patients they have but a few days to live. One such case was with my friend's sister, who was on a life-saving machine. Several times the doctors wanted to unplug it, thinking it was a waste of time. But her son knew the final word was God's, and he adamantly refused to give them the permission. God honored his faith and restored his mother's health. With therapy, she improved and lived about a year longer. The sickness that is dominating your life is a result of your lack of faith in the God who knows your body more than any well-trained doctor.

Today, because of the extent of medical research and advanced technology, doctors are able to diagnose effectively the cause of an illness and treat it at an early stage before it gets out of control. Consequently, people's faith is transferred slowly from God to man. But it is God who has equipped these doctors with the potential to successfully perform any operation. And no matter how good the doctor may be, it is God who will decide whether a patient lives or dies. So, though the doctor may give you a few days to live, it is God who has the final word.

There is no sickness upon the face of this earth that God cannot heal. He knows the structure of your body. He is the designer. It is He who made us, and not we ourselves. As children, my late grandfather hated when we played with dolls. He would say, "Man is trying to make man but he still failed, as he can't blow the breath of life into the doll."

We need to stop petting our illnesses and command them to leave our bodies. When arthritis commands you to sit and not move, stand up in the name of Jesus and claim your healing. It may sound very strange, but if you believe with all your heart that God can heal you, you will be healed. The healing process may sometimes take a little time, as only God can determine when He wants you healed. But make sure that during the waiting period, you do not lose faith. Simply say, "Yes Lord, I know healing is on the way, and I thank you."

As I told you before, when I felt the tremor in my feet, I said, "God, you know my body more than I do. You have the power to heal me and, based on that fact, I trust you right now to touch my body." And yes, I have seen results.

I have heard over and over again of people who were healed after doctors pronounced their conditions permanent. One such situation was published in a well-known newspaper which told the story of a man who was blinded as a result of an accident encountered on his job. Doctors tried desperately to restore his sight, but without success. One day while in church, he was reminded of God's power to heal. That day he decided not to go home until he was healed. The church became his home and after about fifteen months, he received his miraculous healing. Today, he is a prominent businessman in Manhattan.

God still heals today. Some Christians will tell you that they don't believe in miracles; that miracles only happened in Bible days. But I can assure you that God never changes. He is the same yesterday, today, and forevermore. He is alpha and omega, the beginning and the end, the first and the last; there is no one to be compared with Him.

Don't go around blaming God for your sickness. Blame your negligence in taking care of your body. How many times were you told that certain foods were not good for you? Now diabetes takes over your body and you blame God for what happened to you. If it were left up to God alone, you would have been fine. Don't give in to your sickness. Don't allow it to dictate what you do from what you don't do; don't make it the God of your life. The commandment says, "Thou shalt have no other God beside me."

Give God a chance to work through you and for you. As the song goes,

Let the Lord have his way,
In your life every day,
There's no joy, there's no place,
Until the Lord has his way,
He will give you command
So let the Lord, let the Lord have the way.

Yield to Him your lack, and let Him have dominion over the sickness that's been plaguing you all your life. He is your healer.

No Money—It's Your Lack

One of the lessons I have learned from owning a home is that, once you have been given the dream, you also have been given the resources to fulfill the dream. At first when I was asked by Mr. Bullock if I loved the house, my response was "Yes, but I don't have any money." But as soon as I decided in my heart to own the house, money was no longer the problem. All it takes is faith and proper planning. So if you have no money in your pocket, don't blame your circumstances, don't blame your parents, don't blame the financial institutions, don't blame your lack of opportunity, blame yourself for not attacking your lack.

The wise man Solomon tells us in Proverbs 20:11 that, "If you love to sleep, you will end in poverty. Keep your eyes open, and there will be plenty to eat!" I have noticed that a lot of our young men, for example, place little interest in acquiring a good education and, as a result, become stagnant in growth and have no job and no money. Many times they are seen on the street corners in groups gambling or engaging in drugs and idle talk. For them, poverty will walk their path until they decide to get up and change the direction of their lives in a positive way.

What about your dream of becoming a singer? What have you done with it? Have you buried it? Do you know that could be the avenue through which you'll have money in your pocket? The rich do not sit down and wish for things to happen. They make things happen. They are risk- takers. They do not hesitate to put their ideas into action. I have heard of one who started a business in his garage with two hundred dollars that he borrowed from his father. You need to get up from where you are and start doing something. If you don't have money, it is your lack.

And if you once had it and don't anymore, it is still your lack. You need to practice the art of budgeting. Good planning is necessary for money to be constantly in your pocket. Don't try to be like the Joneses, thinking that you have to have the same name-brand shoes as they. Instead, invest wisely. If you want to be successful, you have to start planning. Learn to put first things first. Don't spend on things that you have no need of. Instead, put that money away in your savings so you have it for future use. In Jamaica, this is referred to as saving for Mr. Rainy Day.

Give and it shall be given. The more you give, the more you receive. Some people prefer to save all they have and ignore the needs of others. But if you learn to spread your wealth, very soon you will have to expand your store house. As Adolto Prieto said, "All the gold in the world has no significance. That which is lasting are the thoughtful acts which we do for our fellow man."

Chapter Fifteen

It's All a Part of God's Will

For we know that all things work together for good to them that love the Lord and are called according to his purpose.

Romans 8:28

Our journey in life is not always easy. Our burdens are sometimes too heavy to carry; our sorrows are unbearable; we do not always get what we want no matter how hard we've tried. We sometimes make wrong decisions that affect our journey for the rest of our lives. Sometimes we are happy, sometimes we are sad. We never can be totally contented at any one stage of our lives. When we have plenty, we complain; when we have little, we complain, and on and on we go, trying to reach our final destination.

Many times we question, "Lord, why is it so hard? Why couldn't it be a little easier? Why do I have to carry the burden I now have? Why?" And on and on we go, trying to understand everything that happens in our lives. But no matter how hard we've tried, there are some things that we will never understand, and no matter how hard we've tried to make things work, there are things that never will work. Why? Because they may not be a part of God's plan for our lives. He is in control. There are things that He gives us control over, and others He chooses to control, for He is God.

The atheist will tell you that there is no God; the scientist will try to explain everything scientifically, but no matter how hard they've tried, there are some things they will never understand.

When the Challengers Gospel Band was functional, there was one song we sang that I love very much. The words go like this:

There are things that a man can do,
He can sail through the air in his plane,
Though man can do a lot of things,
Man He is limited.
(Tell me) Can you catch the wind,
Can you make the world spin,
Can you pull the sun down,
Can you make man from the ground,
Oh no but I know who can
God can, God can.

God is the director of our lives. He is in control and whatever happens is all part of God's plan. As a result, it makes no sense when we murmur and complain and wish things were otherwise. Every experience that we've been through, whether good or bad, has a purpose in our lives. Sometimes it is to teach us lessons we will need for the future. Sometimes it is to point us in the right direction; sometimes it is just a reminder of who God is. So don't take them lightly.

God knows our journey more than we do. He knows every roadblock, every trap, every pothole, and every attack that we will face. He is always ahead of us and wants to lead us on a safe path. Sometimes He will instruct us to divert, for there is danger just around the corner. Listen to him when he speaks. Thank him for everything that happens in your life. The psalmist says in Psalms 37:23-24, "The Lord directs the steps of the godly. He delights in every detail of their lives.

Though they stumble, they will not fall, for the Lord holds them by the hand."

The Architect of Your Life

It is not wise to build a house without a plan. As a matter of fact, it is a requirement in most countries to present a blueprint of your plan to relevant authorities. The plan should give every detail of the building you hope to construct. Most times this is done by an architect who is trained in the field. Every detail is necessary: the size of the building, the number of doors, windows, the form, structure, and so on. The more knowledgeable the architect, the better will be your blueprint, hence the final product: your house.

God is the architect of our lives. He knows our blueprint even before we were born. He knows every victory we will experience, every mountain we will climb; every Red Sea we will cross; every desert we will go across. He knows what we can bear and what we can't. As a result, He made us who we are, put us where we are, gave us what we have—talents and abilities—every building block, every window that we need to build our lives, he has given to us, even the workmanship that we will need. It could be our parents, our environment, our pastors, our teachers, our friends, our enemies, our employers, every person that's needed to help us build, God has provided.

Some elements of our building cannot be done where we are and, as a result, God sends us to various places and take us from one stage to another. Sometimes we have to go through the fiery furnace, sometimes through the cold, sometimes through the tunnel. But rest assured that God is the best architect of your life and where He sends you, where you are, is exactly where you should be until the mission is completed.

I came to the United States at a time when I was struggling with a lot of problems. Financially, I could not see my way out. All doors seemed closed, except this one. The decision was not an easy one, as I had to give up a job I had had for ten years, a senior teacher's position I had had for eight years, I would be separated from my children, leave my house, and, in the process, would lose all that I owned. But during my time here, I realized that God was in it; that God was preparing me for the task he had for me; that he was refining me to be gold with value.

The experience was not an easy one, but through it all I have learned to trust God more; I have discovered abilities that I never thought I had, such as writing this book, editing a newspaper, and co-hosting a radio program. I have come to understand that God is the architect of my life and that whatever He has done is well done. Whatever blessing He has given you, no one can take away; whatever door he has closed, stays closed, no one can open it. Through this experience, I have learned to move with the flow of what I have no control over and let God have his way.

Though I miss my children, I know that God is in it and when the time is right for us to be reunited, it will happen and no one can stop it. Not only has God continued to lead my life, but that of my ex-husband and children. Though they have gone through a lot, each experience will help them to be better people in the future. David, while tending his father-in-law's sheep, learned to conquer lions with his bare hands. It was God preparing him for the task of killing Goliath and conquering all the enemies he would come upon in his path through life.

You may be wondering what are you doing where you are now, but don't forget for one moment "that things work together for good to them that loved the Lord and are called according to his purpose." (Rom. 8: 28) For every step you take in life, thank God for each step and depend on him to direct you along. He will give you the strength to go through your hard times: financial, abuse, addiction, a wrong choice, a poor decision, whatever it may be. Life is a gamble: sometimes we win, sometimes we lose. But losing is not always bad, as it prepares us for a better comeback.

Right now God is in the process of developing your design to make you more attractive and marketable. He is right now preparing you to be what He desires you to be: a better father, a better mother, a better daughter, a better son, a better employer or employee, to be better at your finances, to be a better planner. He may be preparing you for a career that will bring you more fulfillment. Psalms 37:7 says, "Be still in the presence of the Lord and wait patiently for Him," for he is the architect of your life.

He Is in Control

The saying goes in Jamaica, "Man a plan, God a wipe out." Whether you agree or not, God is in control. You can make all the plans you want, but remember God has the final say. He is the God of the universe. He is in control. How many times has the meteorologist predicted bad weather for a particular day which turns out to be the best day for a picnic! Man has limited knowledge, but with God there is no limit. He is referred to as the Universal Intelligence.

When my father has an appointment and he dreams ripeness the night before, he knows that he will succeed at whatever the appointment is. But when he dreams green, he knows he's up for some disappointment.

In Jamaica, it is everybody's dream to get a VISA to come to the United States. No matter what he/she has to do, he/she goes with determination to get it, especially because the fee is so expensive. But no matter the level of determination, if the interviewer is not satisfied with your reason for the visit, you will not get it. I have seen people distraught as a result of not receiving their VISA. But if it were God's will for that person to get the VISA, no matter the frame of mind of the interviewer or what documents he has in front of him, the interviewee would receive it.

The quicker we accept the fact that God is in control, the better we will be able to accept the challenges in our lives. You may be a health-conscious person and the first time you go to the doctor for a check-up, you are diagnosed with cancer of one kind or another.

I know a lady who was in her mid-eighties and rarely saw the doctor, as she assumed she was in perfect health. One day, for whatever reason, she decided to visit the doctor, only to be told her prognosis showed that her entire body was infested with cancer. She lived for about two months after that visit.

There are times when we take things for granted. We get up in the morning, thinking, “Hey, another day for work.” We do not even pause to say, “Thank you Lord for the opportunity to live.” We sometimes behave as though we have our lives in control. We can do as we like, as we owe no one any obligation. But let me remind you that God has your life in control. It is His decision as to how long you will stay in this world, not the doctors. Though you may try to avoid Him at times, He often puts us through a crisis to remind us of who He is and what He can do. He demands we have total reliance on Him.

I admire a particular friend who makes it her habit to consult God about everything she is about to do. If she is going to the hair salon, she asks God’s direction and, hey, she is right—anything can happen when she goes there.

I remember one night coming from a meeting at Siloah New Testament Church in Jamaica. After walking about a mile, I became very tired and, soon after, I recognized a friend driving towards me. I was so happy and got in the van. He had not even driven ten chains when he began to lose control of the vehicle and it started to climb the embankment. I never felt so scared in my life!

No matter how good a plan we have in life, if God is not a part of it, then it is no plan at all. We have to recognize Him as the God in control; the God who can bring us blessings or curses. The psalmist must have recognized the difference when things were placed in the hands of the Lord when he said in Psalms 37:5 “Commit everything you do to the Lord. Trust in him and he will help you.”

In 2010, when the great earthquake hit Haiti, it was the worst catastrophe in a long time. Thousands of people lost their lives. But I would imagine that no one could have predicted this as so many people were busy doing what they normally did. Though I sympathized with my brothers and sisters, it was a reminder to all of us who God is—not a cruel God, but one who is merciful and in control.

When God instructs you to go on a journey, do not allow fear and those who think they always know best, prevent you from starting your journey. Though you may not be sure where you are going or why you are going, rest assured that God is in control and you will fear no evil for He is with you. As soon as you obey and take your first step, the Lord will open your eyes to the reason for the journey.

Many times when things do not turn out the way we wish, we conclude that it was not the will of God, but I am sure that if God never wanted you to go He would have stopped you before you went, since He is in control. Perhaps He wanted to teach you a lesson or two.

The year when we sat the Common Entrance Examination, most of our teachers thought two of us girls would be successful, but the boy they least expected to pass was the one who was successful. Again, God was in control. If He had wanted us to attend high school (at that time there were secondary and high schools), He would have allowed it. But that was not His plan. He wanted us to go to Maggotty Secondary School. And did we do well? Oh yes we did and were given leadership positions.

Don't go around feeling sorry for yourself. You are right where you are because that's where God intends you to be, and when the time is right, when He is pleased with your progress, He will move you on. At this moment as I write, it is fast approaching six years since I last saw my children, but I know that when God is pleased with me—the end product—He will grant me the opportunity to be with them again.

Give God the glory and the honor due to His name. See Him as the master of your life. Trust Him to work things out for you in His own way and in His own time. He is in control.

Nothing Happens by Chance

Because God is in control, nothing in your life happens by chance, whether it is good or bad. When Joseph's brothers threw him into the pit, they thought they were doing him displeasure, but God meant it for good. When Moses defended his slave brother by killing the attacker, it was an awful thing he did, but God meant it for good. Saul was heading towards Damascus to persecute the Christians when he came face to face with God, and God meant it for good.

All things are allowed in your life for a reason. Nothing happens by chance. You may ask why has God allowed this to happen or why doesn't God prevent this from happening. He did not because He never wanted to. He allowed it for a reason. Sometimes you are not able to tell why, at least not yet, but with time you will look back and say, "Forgive me, God, for doubting that You cared. Thank You for allowing this in my life."

Did I have to spend so long from my children? Yes, because God allowed it. He allowed it for our good. I am not the same as when I left Jamaica. I am stronger spiritually, emotionally, psychologically. I have obtained wisdom in making decisions. I have learned to weigh the pros and cons before I make decisions. I have learned how painful it can be at times to be away from my children. I have learned that sometimes America is not the answer.

You were told in the Scriptures to make your request known, and you may have been praying for God to grant you a special favor. You have prayed about this one thing for many years and have now become discouraged and think that God does not hear you at all. But the truth is, God answers all prayers, but maybe the answer you expect is not the answer He has for you. He may be saying to you, "If I grant your request, you will spend the rest of your life in misery, and I do not want that for you." Or He may be saying, "I want to grant you your request, but now is not the right time. You are not ready yet. I will have to shape you up a little: build your faith, strengthen your character, curb that bad habit of yours, or teach you first how to forgive."

God knows what is best for each of us. We look at the immediate, while He looks way ahead of us. He can see any destruction ahead of us. As a result, when things happen in our lives, they are not by chance.

I heard the story of a woman who had prayed for a long time for God to bless her womb with a child. She and her husband tried everything possible, but pregnancy just never happened. One day she went to a church meeting, and the pastor told her she was going to have many children. (That reminds me of Mary, when the angel told her that she would give birth to a baby, and she said, "How can this thing be?") A short while after the woman gave birth to a child. A year or so after that, she gave birth to twins and continued until she had six beautiful children! Maybe God didn't answer her prayer immediately because she was not ready to receive such a blessing. The waiting period was all a part of God's plan. And when she was ready, He poured out His blessings upon her.

I am the first child of my parents. Four brothers were born after me, and all four died. My other three sisters came after that, and all three are alive and well. I have been asking the question, "Why did God take back my four brothers?" But some things we will never know, at least not yet. But whatever the reason, God knows best and things never happen by chance; everything is part of God's plan.

During my pregnancy with the baby I lost, I was not as sick as when I was pregnant with my other two children. With that pregnancy, I tried to do everything right since I now had more experience. I was told by one teacher that I was the prettiest with this pregnancy. But it didn't matter how careful I was or how healthy, it was not God's will for the baby to be alive. I had a stillbirth. It didn't happen by chance.

At work you may be preparing yourself for a possible promotion, and yet the vacancy is filled by someone else, maybe even a less-qualified person. But don't despair. Don't be discouraged. That promotion at that particular time was not for you. Probably God has something better in store for you. Just simply say to Him, "God, I thank you that I still have your favor on me, and I know that you will bless me when the time is right."

When Monique said to me, "Mom, I want you to come home," she never said it by chance. It probably was God's way of saying, "Yes, Maizie, it's time to go home. My purpose for you being in the United States is accomplished, now it is time to go." Nothing happens by chance.

God is not only interested in the big issues in your life—your need for a child, for a husband/wife, for a promotion—He is also interested in the small issues, such as leaving a phone charger at home when your battery signals a low battery. I was on my way to my job as a caregiver one night when I remembered that I had not put my phone charger in my bag. I looked at my phone and realized I only had one bar, which meant that I would not be able to speak to anyone for the entire week. I do not know why God allowed me to forget it, but I know that it did not happen by chance. He allowed it for a reason. It was a part of His plan. Who knows, He might have been preventing me from a call that would have produced emotional hurt!

You may have an important meeting to attend and are in great hurry, as you do not want to be late. But as you get on the highway, you realize that traffic is going really slowly and there's no way you can prevent being late to that meeting. But instead of getting upset, give God thanks for having control of everything. He knows why you are delayed. It never happens by chance.

Do you know that there is a reason for the people you meet from day-to-day? Nothing happens by chance. God controls the universe which is comprised of energies and attractions. We are all connected, and sometimes the answers to our prayers are revealed through someone we've met before. A friend of mine was coming from work one particular day when she bumped into a former schoolmate she had not seen for many years, but God would have it that way. It never happened by chance as God used that gentleman to open doors for me that I never thought possible.

I have heard of a young lady who met her husband by way of colliding into him at a supermarket as they were going through the door. One was coming out while the other was going in. And that was how they met. Shortly afterwards, they were married. When you allow God to control your life, nothing will happen by chance. He sometimes does things to slow us down or to prevent us from danger; sometimes to instruct us as to what course to take in life; sometimes it is simply to remind us of who He is.

Continue to give him the praise and the honor due to His name, especially when things do not turn out the way you want them to. Trust Him to work for you and through you. He knows everything that is best and will allow nothing in your life without a reason. Everything will be according to His will.

Chapter Sixteen

Give God the Praise

Praise ye the Lord. Praise, O ye servants of the Lord, praise the name of the Lord.

Psalm 113:1

A former pastor must have caught the vision when he instructed us to give words of encouragement to any speaker who delivered God's message to us. He realized that encouragement in the form of praise has power to bring out the best in any person. The problem, however, is when we allow the praise to go to our heads! We take all the praise for ourselves and forget to pass it on to the God, who enabled and empowered us to do what we did. Whenever I am praised in any form, my response is, "Thank you." But quietly in my heart I will say, "God, I praise you. I could not have done it on my own, so it has to be you, Lord."

A friend of mine once asked me, "Girl, how do you find it so easy to forgive?" I said to him, "It's not me, but the Christ who lives in me." As Christians, many of the things required of us cannot be done if God is not in us. Without him, we can do nothing.

Praising God is an act of faith. We are actually saying to him, "Thank you, God, for who you are and for what you have already done and for what you are about to do." Praise brings God honor and glory. David says in Psalm 113:1, "Praise ye the

Lord. Praise, O ye servants of the Lord, praise the Lord." It is hoped that at the end of this chapter you will see the value of praise and that it may be employed to bring richness to your life.

The Power of Praise

I heard the story once of a rapist who broke into a woman's house with the intention of raping her. When she realized the danger she was in, she began to praise God. The rapist got so confused that he shouted at her to keep quiet, but the more he shouted, the more the woman praised God. And though he threatened to kill her, she continued to praise God. The rapist became so terrified and powerless that he left the house faster than he had come.

There is power in praise. When you give praise to God, things will never be the same. In Bible days—though the same may be happening in some prisons today—the prisons were always in a dilapidated condition and devoid of the most basic comforts. Such was the condition of the prison Paul and Silas were in, although they did nothing wrong; they were innocent of the charge. But Acts 16 tells us that at midnight, Paul and Silas began to sing praises to God. Suddenly, there was a massive earthquake and the prison was shaken to its foundation. The doors flew open, their chains fell off, and they, along with the other prisoners, could have escaped, but they did not. When the guard saw what had happened, he thought all the prisoners had escaped. He drew his sword and was ready to kill himself, until Paul shouted at him not to bring any harm to himself. The guard then asked, "What must I do to be saved?" That's what praise can do. It will break the chains of captivity and set you free.

You may not be bonded by physical chains. It may be the chain of an abused relationship, the chain of inadequate finances, the chain of drug abuse, or alcohol addiction. Give God praise each time you are tempted to sit in your chains, and watch God bring the deliverance and self-restoration that you need to overcome. Watch Him bring you the finances you need to pay the debt that has burdened you for most of your life. Watch him restore the broken relationship and bring back the joy and happiness you once experienced.

When God is praised, He draws closer to you. He will come to your rescue as he did for that lady, as well as for Paul and Silas. As a matter of fact, in the Old Testament, when the enemies were arrayed against Judah, King Jehoshaphat sent the choir ahead of the army to praise God! It may seem like a crazy thing to do, but the truth is, it worked. The enemy's army was led into ambush and was defeated.

If you want to have victory over the enemy, start to praise God. I remember when I was younger, and sickness came upon any member of the church, the prayer warriors would go down into prayer and fast and sing praises unto God. On one such occasion, a church brother was sick unto death and my mother led her team into prayer and fasting. They started praise God for healing the brother, and today he is alive and well. Don't allow the devil to defeat you. Start praising God, and He will draw closer to you to give you the victory that you need. Praise does not come naturally when you are down and depressed. But praising God has nothing to do with how you feel; when you don't feel like doing it, that's when you need to do it the most. I found out that during those moments when I lift up my voice and praise God, I find strength that I never thought I had. Praise is the channel through which God enters your problems and bring solutions you never thought possible.

Instead of going around complaining about how unfair life is, start praising God that you have life! Give him praise and honor. When your enemy comes upon you, lift your hands and praise God. David had many enemies, but each time he was attacked he gave praises to God, and from this he found the strength to fight victoriously. He says in Psalm 68:19 "Praise the Lord, praise God our Savior! For each day he carries us in his arms."

Don't allow the cares of life to press you down. Give praise to God. Each time you think that your spouse is unfaithful, give praise to the Lord; when your children turn their backs on you, give God the praise; when your boss tells you that your service is no longer needed, give God the praise. When your friends fail you, give God the praise. When your problems soar higher than the mountain, give God the praise. He will bring you deliverance. Let God's praise be in your heart at all times.

How to Praise God

I usually say to my mathematics students that there are many ways to find solutions to problems, though there is only one solution. The same is true with praise. There are many ways to give praise to God, of which I'm about to explore.

God can be praised through your songs. Throughout the Psalms, singing is the most popular form of praise, maybe because David was a musician. I find that when I am faced with any crisis, and I choose to sing praises to God, I am overwhelmed with joy and peace. Or I may put in one of my favorite CDs and play it, which also brings comfort and peace. Psalm 57:7 (NLT) says "My heart is confident in you. Oh God, my heart is confident in you. Oh God, my heart is confident." No wonder I can sing your praises.

When the cares of life tend to press me down I sing,

> I've never had a prayer that God couldn't answer,
> I've never shed a tear he could not dry,
> And when the waves of life are so high that I can't mount them,
> He will roll me over the tide.

What sweet relief it brings! When the choir lifts its voice in melody and sings,

> I've found a friend in Jesus,
> He's everything to me,

He's the fairest of ten thousand to my soul,
He is the beautiful Rose of Sharon,
He's all the world to me,
But best of all he is my coming King.

Joy filled the heart of the lonely.

When you are down and out, choose a song that speaks to you, and lift your voice to the Lord. I remember my mother could be heard singing over the washtub. If she was not singing, she would be humming. It must have given her the strength to go through the dark moments of her life, and it will do the same for you, too.

While you are singing, you can further enhance your singing with your hands. When the children of Israel came across the Red Sea, they lifted their voices, knocked their tambourines, and no doubt clapped their hands. I have a problem with churches that see this as a disturbance. I love to make a joyful noise unto the Lord. David says in Psalm 68:24-27 (NLT)

> Your procession has come into view. Oh God, the procession of my God and King as he goes into the sanctuary. Singers are in front, musicians behind, between them are young women playing tambourines. Praise God, all you people of Israel, praise the Lord, the source of Israel's life. Look, the little tribe of Benjamin leads the way.

Praising God with our hands does not only mean that we lift them up to Him, it also means when we use them to do well unto others. Giving the lonely and depressed a hug may bring life and assurance that all is not lost, that somebody still cares. A hug from a friend when we are going through our dark moments means a lot. It brings warmth, love, and happiness. I can understand why some people commit suicide during holidays when they have no one to share those moments with. So start right now by praising God with your hands.

Another way in which you can praise God is through your words. David says, "Thy word have I hid in my heart that I may not sin against thee." Colossians 3:17 says "And whatever you do in word and deed do it as a representative of the Lord Jesus Christ, giving thanks through him to God the Father."

In an earlier chapter I spoke about the power of words. When we use them to put others down, we are certainly not praising God. When we use them to lie and cheat, we are not praising God. But quite the contrary, when we use words to bring glory to God, we are praising him. When we use them to lift others up, we are praising God. When we use them to correct others in a loving manner, we are praising God. When we speak words of wisdom and faith, we are praising God. When we use them to defend ourselves against Satan, we are praising God. That's what Jesus did when he was tempted by the devil. So when sickness takes hold of your body and Satan keeps reminding you that the doctor says you only have a few days to live, tell him, "Satan, you are a liar. Sickness has no control of my body and my God has the final words, not the doctor." That's praising God.

When you tell others what God has done for you, that's praising God. That is why testimony is so important. When Jesus ministered to the woman of Samaria, she ran to tell others about it. She said, "Come see a man who told me all things." Many times when Jesus healed others, they would go and tell their stories.

People today are afraid to tell what God has done for them. Testimony now seems a thing of the past. In church, instead of people giving their personal experience of how God came through for them at some point in their lives, they choose to repeat the testimony given by others in a song! How do we expect others to come to Christ when we keep quiet about what God has done for us? God is good and worthy of all our praise.

I remember once on my Christian pathway I lost touch with God. I was not feeling Him as I used to. But during a weekend retreat, God allowed me the opportunity to confess my all to

Him and to pick up my broken pieces. I handed all my troubles over to Him and he did wonders with them. He put them back together, and I moved back in fellowship with Him. I was never the same again.

When I shared how God provided a home to me without a cent in my hand, the faith others had in God increased. When I tell of writing this book, which I can only do through Christ, I'm encouraging others to go for their dreams, to maximize the potential God has given them. And that's praising God. So don't be afraid to open your mouth and talk about God and His goodness.

Our feet can be used to praise God, even if it is simply to stomp them to the tune of a song in your heart. I may be in a place where I can't sing, but I can make joyful sounds with my feet.

Telling others about the love of God should not be limited to Saturday or Sunday worship. It should be every day, every hour, minute, or second. Go across to your neighbor and say, "God loves you." This is praising God. Visiting the sick and those in prison is praising God. Jesus was always busy doing His Father's will on earth and so should we. That's why He saved us, so that we can help others to experience His blessings now and after this life.

Did you know that God can be praised with your stomach? When we rid ourselves of unhealthy food and toxic substances, we are praising God. That's taking care of our bodies and that's praising God. When the Hebrew boys in Daniel, Chapter 1, refused to partake of the King's table, they were praising God. Many times we allow our stomachs to be our God! Praise God with your stomach and be blessed with a good and prosperous life. Obesity will never be a game you have to play.

God can be praised in our thoughts. Remember, "As a man thinketh, so is he." You are your thoughts. Mark 12:30 says "Love the Lord with all your heart, and with all your soul, and with all your strength." Allowing the mind of Christ to be in you, is giving praise to God. Everything we do is as a result of our thoughts; hence, if Christ occupies our thoughts wherever we are, then we are praising God.

Why Should You Praise God

In church when people are asked to give testimony, many say, "When I think of the goodness of Jesus and what He has done for me, my soul cries out *hallelujah*, thank God for saving me." But God saving you is not the only reason to praise him. There are many other reasons. As the song says, "To write the love of God would drain the ocean dry." I can only explore a few reasons why we should praise God.

- ***He is the Creator.*** Isaiah 66:1-2 states, "This is what the Lord says: Heaven is my throne, and the earth is my footstool. Could you build me a temple as good as that? Could you build such a resting place? My hands have made both heaven and earth; they and everything in them are mine. I, the Lord, hath spoken!" All creation is called upon to praise God, for he is the Creator. When we examine the fact that God spoke this world into existence and made man from the dust of the earth, we ought to bow down and worship him. Without him, we would be nothing. We are not our own. We are his. He put us here and will take us when He is ready. So, every day, it is our duty to give praise to God.
- ***For his wisdom.*** God has infinite wisdom. As wise as man thinks he is his, wisdom cannot be compared with the wisdom of God. In Daniel 2:20 Daniel says, "wisdom and might are his." That is why we can relax in Him, assured of the fact that He knows all things and will use His infinite wisdom to lead and direct us on life's journey.

- ***For his greatness.*** When we look back on all that God has done for us, we can truly say that God is great. Each time we hear the thunder rolls, we can say God is great; at night when we look in the sky and how well lit the heavens are, we can say God is great; bringing the forces of the universe to bring our dreams to fruition, we can say God is great. Sometimes God brings people from afar, people we are not acquainted with, to bring solutions to our problems; God is great. Psalm 145:3 says, "Great is the Lord! He is most worthy of our praise! No one can measure his greatness." When Harvard University neurosurgeon Dr. Carson separated the Siamese twins, he did a great work. But he recognized the fact that it could not have been done without God working with him. God is to be praised.
- ***For he is holy.*** Exodus 15:11 says, "Who is like you among the gods, oh Lord-glorious in holiness, awesome in splendor, performing great wonder? There is none who is as holy as God." That's why we are instructed to, "Be holy, as I am holy." His holiness demands our respect and honor. And if Christ is in our lives, we must live holy lives.
- ***For his faithfulness.*** He is a God of his words. Whatever he has promised, that's what He will do. I reflect on the story of Jacob and Esau. Though Esau has the birthright, being the firstborn, God has promised to bless Jacob, and that's a promise he keeps. Isaac was blind and thought that God was blessing Esau, but it was a part of God's plan. God never goes back on his promises. When things don't go your way, praise God, for He is faithful and just in bringing forth that which you desire—and it will be done in His own time and in His own way. He promised never to leave you nor forsake you, and He

> will remain faithful to His words, even when things around are indicating the opposite. God is an awesome God and, as a dear friend of mine said, "When God works, you always have to be in awe, for he is great and specializes in things thought impossible."

Give God the honor and praise due unto His name and watch Him unfold blessings in your life. You will have doors open that you never thought would open, windows opened that you thought impossible, rivers crossed that you thought were not crossable, dreams fulfilled that you thought were unattainable. Praise him in the morning, at noontime, and in the evening. Praise Him all the day long, for He is worthy to be praised.

Part Four

A Better You

Chapter Seventeen

Love Yourself

> *My dove is hiding behind the rocks, behind an outcrop of cliff. Let me see your face; let me hear your voice. For your voice is pleasant, and your face is lovely.* Songs of Solomon 2:14, NLT

In his book, *How to Get What You Want and Keep What You Have*, John Gray tells us of the seven love tanks that we all have to fill from time to time. I find it very informative, especially where he speaks of self-love—referred to as Vitamin S—which comes before Vitamin R (Romance and Relationships). According to John, if the Vitamin S tank is empty, then we may never be successful at relationships or romance. In other words, you can't love anyone if you are not able to love yourself.

If we should pause and examine our failed relationships, we would discover that sometimes the root of the problem is an inability to love ourselves. Apart from not being able to love anyone, we are emotionally incapable of giving and receiving love. We feel we are empty of giving love. Our self-esteem deteriorates, and our self-image, which according to Dr.Schuller is "The inner program that charts our course, determines or predetermines our reactions to what happens to us—," will be blurred by our inadequacies, faults, and mistakes. We will have difficulty forgiving ourselves and, as a result, feel that we are not worthy to be in the land of the living. Happiness, contentment, and peace of mind evade us, and all we feel is resentment, hatred, and self-pity. We always come out being the victim, which is a sad state for us to be in.

God loves us with an everlasting love and has given us everything we need to love ourselves. So let us not think that we are selfish when we fall in love with ourselves for, according to Sam Keen, author of *Love and be Loved,* "Loving yourself requires the same kind of commitment and vows as do a marriage. Promise to love and cherish all parts of yourself until death do us part." Without self-love we will not be able to love others, love God, or His creation. We will continue to find fault in ourselves, others, and the universe in general.

If you are in a relationship in which you think you are not getting enough love or attention, check your self-love tank to see if it is empty. Start to pay attention to yourself. Go on the vacation you have always wanted to go on; visit the beauty salon and make yourself as beautiful as you can; go for the career you've always wanted. Just spend some time loving yourself, and you will find love flowing in your relationship again. Many times we find ourselves too busy attending to others and forget that we need attention, too.

One day during the summer of 2008, while I was in the United States, I decided to spend some time with myself. I went to a particular restaurant, sat down, and the waitress walked over with the menu. When she was ready to take my order, she asked me, "Are you alone?" I politely and enthusiastically answered, "Yes, I am." She looked at me, smiled, and then walked away. She returned a few minutes later with my order, and I asked her, "Do you think a woman can enjoy a meal by herself?" Again she smiled. I enjoyed my meal while listening to a live band playing the best of Bob Marley. That was one of the best days of my life. On that particular day, I could have stayed home and felt sorry for myself, thinking how unfair life is, but I refused to travel that route. I refused to play the part of the victim. I loved myself too much for that to happen.

One day I told a friend that I went to the movies by myself. She responded, "Are you crazy? Can a woman go to the movies by herself?" Oh, yes! I am not saying that if you feel like hanging around home it is a sign of lack of self-love. Instead, what I am saying is that sitting at home feeling sorry for yourself because no one loves you enough to take you out is a sign of lack of self-love. You do not want to fall into this state. It is like putting an end to your life while you are still alive.

Being away from my family on Christmas 2008, I decided to enjoy Christmas by myself. My employer found it funny when I told him I would be by myself. But that year, you never would have believed I wasn't expecting visitors, as I did all the same things I would do if I had visitors. I prepared a lovely breakfast and dinner, played music and danced, and then I sat down and watched movies. Was it a good day? Oh sure! It was the best Christmas I've had in the United States.

The bottom line is that you need to spend time with yourself and enjoy it as much as you would if somebody were with you. Stop wallowing in self-pity when a man does not turn up to take you to the movies or wherever. Entertain yourself. Spend quiet time alone to rejuvenate yourself. Though you may be given a negative label, make a conscious effort not to allow it to make you feel sorry for yourself. Rise above that level and spring forward with new energy to love yourself more than you ever have.

Change What Can Be Changed

As with any other thing, change can be very painful and time-consuming. But with effort and persistence, you will receive a rich reward. Change cannot happen overnight. If all these years you have been living in self-pity, what makes you think that after reading this chapter you will miraculously develop self-love? It won't happen overnight. You will have to make a conscious, persistent, and controlled effort to affect change in your life, and urgency is a necessity.

Starting with an inventory of *who* you are and *where* you are at this moment is important. You must agree on what you want to change and there can be no doubt in your mind. You will have to exercise faith in your ability to change. For instance, if you are abusive, and realize that you have to make a change, first you must know that you want to change and need it desperately. Second, you must believe in your ability to change, no matter the obstacles in your path.

During the short time I worked in the storehouse at Appleton Sugar Factory, I realized the significance of taking inventory. It was a difficult task at first, especially because I was not familiar with the different stock. But with time I learned. I had to take an inventory of the stock to keep abreast of it and make orders when necessary. Was it an easy task? No. But it helped in the smooth operation of the factory.

Are you satisfied with where you are in life? Are you satisfied with your achievements? Are you fulfilling your purpose in life? What is your present standing with your Creator? If He should call on you today, would He be proud of you? Would you be proud of yourself or would you hang your head in shame and think what a failure you have been? If your level of satisfaction is below an acceptable rate, then you need to do something urgently. If your present situation does not make you feel good about yourself, then it is time to do something. You need to start making changes in your life. You need to start thinking about yourself. Every man will have to give an account of himself, whether good or bad, so make sure your account is good. Make sure you hear, "Well done, thou good and faithful servant."

Since change starts in the mind, you have to first start with an evaluation of your thoughts. What thoughts are you thinking right now? Are you thinking how worthless and unattractive you are? Are you at present comparing yourself with your friend wishing that you were more like him/her? Are you thinking that you have no valuable contribution to make to society? Or are you at present wearing the label of no-good that you were given at elementary school?

You have the power to change any negative thoughts that hold you in captivity. The remote control is in your hand. Just as you change the television program that you don't wish to see, you can do the same with the thoughts you do not wish to entertain. Develop the habit of positive self-talk. For each negative thought that wants to take dominance, quickly replace it with a positive thought. For instance, you may presently be thinking how unworthy you are of love. Replace that thought by reminding yourself of how valuable you are; that you are loved by the one who created you; that you are so special that He chose you and equipped you with the special task of making a difference in this world. Remind yourself that you are one of a kind. There is none like you and never will be. You are beautiful, and you are what you are on the inside, not what you are on the outside. Be proud of yourself. Look in the mirror and talk to yourself. I do that sometimes. I will look and say, "Girl, do you know how beautiful you are? You are special."

In taking an inventory of yourself, you may want to examine your relationship with God. This cannot be over-emphasized. It is important to develop a relationship with God, since He is your inventor and knows your self-worth. Allow Him to navigate your life. When you are walking in the shadow of death, you will fear no evil, for He will be with you. He is the best navigator for your life.

Accept That Which Can't Be Changed

Accepting yourself can only be achieved when you have learned to love yourself for who you are. Reading the chapter "Who are You" will help you to appreciate and love yourself. Just as it is important to know the person you intend to spend the rest of your life with, so it is important to know who you are.

Take time to discover your talents. What are you good at doing? Find what you love to do and make it a part of your life. Enjoy it and be the best that you can ever be. Use it to enrich your life and to enhance the lives of others. If you are good at knitting, knit a runner for a friend. If you are good at cooking, invite some friends over for dinner. If you are good at singing, find an avenue where you can inspire others. Don't tell yourself that you are good at nothing, for it is not true. That is a lie from the pit of hell! Everybody has something that he/she is good at doing. Find it and develop it. The more you use what you have, the better you will be at it.

Go for your dreams. Don't allow fear to take hold of you. Others have done it and you can, too. Your dreams are uniquely yours. God has given you that idea and wishes for you to use it to enhance His creation. Don't forget that you are co-creator with God. Don't take these dreams lightly. Go for them now. You may need to go back to the chapter "Go for Your Dreams."

Don't fall into the habit of comparing yourself with others. In his book *To Love And Be Loved,* Sam Keen postulates, "In the degree that we compare ourselves to others and feel that we fall short in creativity, beauty, power, wealth, health, luck, fame or intelligence, we are tempted to want those who appear to have what we lack." So the golden rule is, do not compare yourself with others. There is only one you and no matter how hard you try, you can never be the other person. So don't try to be like your neighbor or your friend, for you never will be. Don't try to be like Michael Jackson, for you never will be. Be yourself. That's all you can ever be. No one shares the same life story as you. None has the passion, the greed, the love, the compassion, the sensuality, the pleasure, or the fears that you have. Dr. Wayne Dyer has this to say, "When you love and trust yourself, you're loving and trusting the wisdom that created you, and when you fail to love and trust yourself, you're denting that infinite wisdom in favor of your ego."

In accepting and loving yourself, do not allow self-pity to cause you to take abuse from anyone. Do not allow yourself to be used as an object, for you are not. You are God's special handmaiden, not to be battered and bounced around like a ball. Self-love will tell you enough is enough. Don't allow anyone to think that they own you, for they do not. You are God's property and should be treated with love and respect. When you are abused, the same is happening to your creator for you are a part of Him. If anyone should mistreat something that you cherish, whether it is a piece of jewelry or a pet, how do you respond? I am sure you will not take kindly to it. So why should you allow anyone to mistreat you? Don't you value yourself?

Set boundaries for yourself. The boundaries must be kept sacred and should not be violated by anyone. When I was a freshman in college, there were certain places you were not allowed to go. You were not allowed to walk across the lawn, and if you did and were caught, you were obligated to apologize to your seniors as well as to the lawn! Make sure that your boundaries are known and that no one—absolutely no one—violates them. And if they do, stand your ground and demand the respect that you deserve. People will treat you the way you allow them to.

What you say is what you get. So be careful of what you say or you may not like what you get. Talk positively to yourself. If you underestimate who you are and convince yourself about it, that is exactly what you will get. Constantly tell yourself, "I am me and I am proud to be me, and I don't care what you think of me, for I am me, and I accept me for who I am."

People sometimes become alcoholics, drug addicts, or abusers, because of their inability to accept themselves for who they are. They think that drugs and alcohol will give them the control they desire, or that it will solve the problems they may be going through. But though it may appear to be true, it is far from the truth. Anyone who abuses drugs, alcohol, or people, does not know who they are. They are walking in the shadow of somebody else. Accepting those things about yourself that you can't change, acts as a terminator of self-destructive thoughts. In accepting yourself, be as truthful as you possibly can. Express your true feelings and don't say you are okay when you are not. You have a right to be angry, but "be angry and sin not."

Stay focused on what you hope to achieve. Relax and have fun. Don't feel guilty for taking care of yourself. Spend quiet moments with yourself and your Creator and let Him reconstruct you and energize you to continue the journey of life. How often do you service your vehicle? If you don't do it at all, one day you may never be able to move it. The engine may be destroyed. The same with you; you need to be recharged, and who is better to do this than God? If anyone deserves love, it is you.

Take Care of Yourself

In Jamaica, it is said that, "Breath keeps house." Have you ever noticed how dilapidated a house looks soon after it is vacant? Insects and rodents take up residency. The roof starts to fall apart, the walls begin to move away from each other, and soon it is covered with weeds. When I was a child, if I saw such a house, I would walk far from it thinking that it was occupied by a ghost.

As with such a house, if we do not take care of our bodies, they will start to deteriorate and may reach a stage of disrepair. In their book, *Healing Moves,* Carol Krucoft and Mitchell Krucoft write, "Health is much more than just the absence of disease. It is a state of physical, mental, and spiritual balance. A truly healthy person," they write, "has the energy and will to perform the tasks of daily life with joy, as well as the ability to rise to the extra challenges of emergencies."

Your body is the temple of God and should be taken care of with proper nutrition, exercise, and rest. Whatever you do affects your body, mind, and soul. According to Gabriel Cousins, M.D, in his book, *Conscious Eating*, "Particular energies exist within each food that affect our physical functioning, the nature of thoughts, and even the expansion of our consciousness." He went on to explain that vegetarians surpassed meat-eating cultures in art, science, and spiritual development. Those who eat meat are more warlike and angry and more focused on sensual passions while vegetarians increase in spiritual sensitivity and awareness.

If you are to take care of yourself, you have to pay special attention to your diet, eliminating all of those foods that give rise to diabetes, obesity, LDL (low density lipoprotein) cholesterol, triglycerides, and arterial hypertension. All of these are high-risk factors of vascular diseases. Cardiovascular ailments are one of the leading causes of death.

The body is like a machine. Once it stops working, it ceases up. I remember my mother usually greased her sewing machine when it wasn't being used for a while. Exercise is, therefore, very important for the body. So along with proper diet, you have to exercise on a regular basis.

Some of the benefits of exercise are improvement of the powerful systems of the body (cardiovascular, respiratory, musculoskeletal, immune, and endocrine); it strengthens the muscles and makes them stronger for everyday tasks; it improves your appearance and develops flexibility. The more you exercise, the more alert you are. But though exercise is necessary, it should not be overdone.

Chapter Eighteen

Love Others

Beloved let us love one another for love is of God and anyone that loveth is born of God and knoweth God. He that loveth not knoweth not God for God is love.

1 John 4:7-8

I was probably fourteen years old when, on a very hot and fuzzy summer day, Old Maus Jack (in my community older men were referred to as Maus) was working assiduously in his cane field, molding new rows to plant his seedlings for the next sugarcane crop. From my back door, I could see him working away nonstop. Compassion went out for him as I thought how hot and thirsty he must be. I went inside, took some sugar and lemon, and made him a glass of lemonade. With surprise and a look of gratitude in his eyes, he took the glass and said, "Thank you, Miss Harriott. May God bless you." He drank it thirstily with a sense of gratitude. I felt good. Even though it was a small gesture, I was able to quench the thirst of a hard-working gentleman.

Loving others does not necessarily mean giving them big and expensive gifts. It simply means being there for them when they need you. It means accepting them for who they are. It means reminding them of how special they are to you. It means giving of yourself when the need arises.

Jesus demonstrated His love for us by dying on the cross like a thief. He committed no sin of His own, but, because He wanted to restore our relationship with our creator, He sacrificed the splendor of heaven. The scripture says, "Greater love hath no man than this than a man lay down his life for his friends." Over and over in the scriptures, we are encouraged to love one another. 1 John 4:7-8 says, "Beloved let us love one another for love is of God and anyone that loveth is born of God and knoweth God. He that loveth not knoweth not God for God is love." If you can't love those who you see and are among, how can you love God who you can't see? The golden rule says, "Do unto others as you would have them do unto you." What difference it would make in our world today if we should apply this verse to our lives! There would be peace on earth and good will among men. Crime and violence would be on the decrease; parents would demonstrate unconditional love for their children instead of being abusive; spouses would honor their marriage vows and not get involved in extra-marital relationships; the wealth of this land would be shared among men. It would not be a situation where the rich get richer and the poor poorer. Cheating and stealing would not be rampant in our society and resources would not have to be wasted to protect us from terrorist attacks.

Having unconditional love for each other is the only way we can experience true success in this life. We are connected. It does not matter our race or color; we are all connected, and we are required to love one another. When there is no love in our hearts, it signifies an absence of God from our lives.

Have you ever had the experience where you were badly hurt by a friend? All you can feel is the hurt, the pain, the agony, and the betrayal. Can you imagine how it must have felt for Jesus when Judas, the same one who supped and ate with him, gave him the kiss of betrayal? At some point in our lives, we've been betrayed by friends, and the truth is that if it weren't for the love of God in our hearts, we would have nothing to do with them. But that's what it means to have un-conditional love: giving love even when you don't feel like it. But, you know you have to. It is the right thing to do, and a part of you is in the other person. This is what God requires of us. "If you love me keep my commandments." Let us love one another.

He Is Your Brother

The man was attacked by assailants and was stripped of all that he had. He was beaten and left to die by the roadside. Religious leaders approached him but instead of giving him a hand, they walked on the other side of the street. There came a Samaritan who was labeled an outcast, but was consumed with love and compassion for the dying man. He bent down, wiped his wounds, put him on his ass, and took him to the hospital. Wasn't that love?

How many times have we turned blind eyes to the poor and needy? They ask us for a penny to buy something to eat; we instead hurl insults at them. Though they may look worn, tired, and weary, they are our brothers. They may not be able to enjoy the pleasure of a roof over their heads, or the comfort of a warm bed, but they are our brothers. They may have gotten themselves involved in crime and violence, but they are our brothers. They may have lived promiscuously and become victims of HIV or other sexually transmitted diseases, but they are our brothers. We are all connected. We are one. Color, education, riches, and religious affiliation should not separate us from the fact that we are one. If a brother or sister does something wrong, it affects all of us.

Today, advanced technology has made this world into a global community. Whether we are ready to accept it or not, we are one and the same. From the dust we came and to the dust we will return. It is time you seek to help your brothers who are in need. Lend a hand when you can. Give a word of comfort. Visit the sick and share a word of hope. Go to the prisons and help your brothers and sisters to find themselves again. Jesus came that we may have life and have it more abundantly. So, if you have been given the gift of life, help others to be beneficiaries as well.

The story is told of a man who was on his way home when he heard shuffling coming from the nearby bushes. He stopped and listened and heard the tearing of garments and the voice of a woman screaming for help. At that point, he did not know what to do. Should he risk his life and go and help the victim or should he pretend not to hear and move on? He thought silently. He wrestled with these two questions, but realizing there wasn't enough time to ponder them over, he decided to go and assist. The man was suddenly endued with power and was able to wrestle with the attacker who eventually fled the scene. The woman apparently was frightened so she ran and hid behind a tree. The hero, as he would be called today, tried to assure the woman that she was now safe, when he heard her say, "Daddy, is that you?" The father was shocked to discover that the victim was his younger daughter. What if he had followed the voice that tried to convince him to flee? What if he had ignored the urge to help? His daughter would have been raped and possibly killed.

Every person that you have come in contact with was meant to be. The beggar, the drunkard, the abuser, and the murderer—they come into our presence for a reason. Give them a word. Remind them of Jesus' love for them. Do you know what that can do for a soul hanging on to the last straw of life? His hope of living can be restored. Give them a smile. Give them a word of cheer. Such can illuminate the darkness from their hearts and replace it with sunshine and an assurance that all is not lost. They do not have to continue living life as victims of their circumstances.

The beggar at gate beautiful asked for money when he saw Peter and John coming towards him. But Peter, being filled with the power of the Holy Spirit, said to him, "Silver and gold have I none; but such as I have given I thee: In the name of Jesus

Christ of Nazareth rise up and walk." (Acts 3:6 KJV) The man immediately got up and walked. He was given back his life.

Spreading rumor and gossip are not to be named among you. Let the words that escape your lips be words of cheer and comfort, words that will give life and not death, words that will build and not destroy. He is your brother! Why kill him with the hurtful words from your lips? Why judge him before finding out the truth of the matter? Each day of my life I am learning not to judge others lest I be judged. I have found out that a lot of times others are wrongfully judged. As a result, I have made an extra effort not to judge even if I am tempted to. Many beautiful relationships are destroyed by deploying false judgments. We are instructed by Jesus not to judge. The same measure in which we judge others is the same measure in which we will be judged.

When others seek to improve themselves, don't go around criticizing them and allowing jealousy and envy to consume your heart. Wish them the best. Celebrate with them. Be there for them to assist them in whatever way you can. Don't go around thinking of yourself more highly than you ought to think. Don't play the part of a hypocrite, either. Ask God to help you to rejoice when others rejoice and to weep when others weep. In other words, feel their pain and share their joy.

The universe is in abundance, and everything to make you happy is there. Because your brother may be able to pursue a college education does not mean that such opportunity is not there for you, too. Whatever you focus on, that is what you will attract. Focus on jealousy for your brother and jealousy you will attract. But when that happens, you are no longer in control of who you are. You are now giving control to the brother of whom you are jealous. Every success this person achieves will burn you like fire. The more you are burned, the more you seek ways to destroy him.

Joseph's brothers were consumed with jealousy and hatred and, as a result, Joseph was sold to the Ishmaelite. But when you are in right standing with God, he will not allow your enemies to conquer you. What they meant for evil, God meant for good. God used Joseph to provide for his father and brothers when the day of famine came. The saying goes, "When you are digging holes, make sure to dig two." In other words, the trap that you set for another may be the same trap in which you are caught. So be careful, as the seed you sow is the seed you reap and if you live in a glass house don't throw stones.

Give your brothers the same love and respect that you want to be given. Taking advantage of others is setting yourself up to be taken advantage of by another. Give love and love you will receive. I end with a quote from Sam Keen, author of *To Love and Be Loved:* "Love without care is reduced to a trivial sentiment or a momentary lust." Let the love in your heart bear fruits of kindness, care, unselfishness, faith, and love.

Love Your Enemies

Loving our enemies is sometimes the hardest thing to do, especially when we are wrongfully accused. As for me, my tolerance level is very low when a lie is told about me. But for us to live in harmony with ourselves and the world in general, we must be willing to love our enemies in spite of what they do. And to love them, we have to be willing to forgive. That's the only way to walk the higher path of consciousness. But how many of us are willing to forgive? How many of us are willing to let go of the wrong done to us by others?

In Matthew 5:45-48, Jesus says to us, "You have heard that it was said, 'Love your neighbors and hate your enemies.' But I say to you, love your enemies and pray for those who persecute you."

Walking around hating others for the wrong they have done you is giving them control of you: your thoughts and your acts. And this allows you to carry a burden too hard for you to bear.

Everything that happens in this universe is supposed to happen exactly the way it happens. When your friends become your enemies, it was meant to be, and since it was meant to be, Why do we go around carrying the unnecessary burden of un-forgiveness? What we need to do instead is to ask God to give us the strength to love unconditionally, even when it does not seem the right thing to do. When your ego says to you, "No, you can't forgive, because you will appear to be soft and vulnerable," allow the spirit of God to work through you. Dr. Wayne Dyer says in his book *You'll See It When You Believe It*, "Forgiveness says, 'I no longer give you the power to control who I am, how I think, and how I'll behave in the future. I take responsibility for all of that now.'"

Romans 12:17-21 says, "Do not repay anyone evil for evil. Be careful to do what is right in the eyes of everybody. If it is possible, as far as it depends on you, live at peace with everyone. Do not take revenge my friend, but leave room for God's wrath, for it is written, It's mine to avenge; I will repay says the Lord." To the contrary, "If your enemy is hungry, feed him, if he is thirsty give him drink, in doing this you will heap burning coals of fire on his head. Do not be overcome with evil, but overcome evil with good."

There are times when others are judged wrongfully and we make them our enemies when they are. I have had personal experiences when I allowed my judgmental attitude to override the good in me and put others in my black book when they should not be. I sometimes misjudged the motives of others for not keeping a promise or for initiating a rumor. Sometimes the reasons were genuine and could not be avoided, or the rumor was not initiated by whom I thought. But these experiences have taught me to not judge lest I be judged. I have learned to give the other person the benefit of the doubt until proven otherwise. And when I am proven wrong, I do not hesitate to say, "I am sorry." A lot of times the problem does not lie with others but with us.

If your enemy refuses to apologize, even then do not hesitate to forgive. It will set you at peace with yourself, with God, and no doubt with your neighbor. Do not refuse to do good to them.

I remember in eighth grade, a classmate and I had some disagreements. We didn't speak to each other for a long time. But each day I realized the weight was getting too heavy for me. I felt very uncomfortable. I could not have peace with myself, although I was not the one who wronged her. The school year ended with us not speaking to each other. But returning for grade nine, I decided to put an end to this misery. I refused to give control of myself to her. As a result, I looked for every opportunity to speak to her. So when she asked the question in class, "Has anyone a sharpener?" I was the first to say, "Yes I do!" She accepted it and from that day we started speaking to each other again and became very good friends until she left for another school. I felt the weight lifted from me.

Jesus, when he was on the cross, prayed for his enemies so that God would forgive them of their sins for they knew not what they did. Stephen, when he was accused, felt lonely and bewildered and as he was being stoned, he lifted his head towards heaven and said, "Lord, do not hold this sin against them." As he said this, he fell asleep.

Forgiving our enemies takes time. It is a process that will not happen until we are ready to feel the hurt and let go. A tutor I had at college could not let go of the hurt of being sexually molested as a child by her uncle, until she came face to face with the anger she had been experiencing all those years. She then let go of this secret she had carried around and felt a freedom she never knew possible. She took control of her life again and was able to enjoy the things in life that everyone should enjoy.

You can't love your enemies until you are willing to forgive them, but when you do, there are benefits to enjoy:

- It gives you power over them.
- You can't defeat them until you experience this power.
- It preserves your freedom and puts you in control again.

- Your health will be improved.
- It puts you in the path of righteousness.
- You are able to love others as yourself.

If you have fought in your heart against anyone, or if you are walking around with the weight of revenge and hatred towards your enemies, give it to God who is willing to provide you with the strength to do that which He requires of you. Don't be afraid of what others will think of you; they may say you are weak or stupid, but pay them no attention. Do what is right to maintain a good relationship with your God. Love your enemies unconditionally.

Working with Others

No man is an island; no man stands alone. Because of our interconnectedness, we cannot be effective and productive when we work in isolation. We need each other and must learn to work with each other. It is sometimes not easy at all as people have different interests, motives, priorities, personality traits, and ideals, but if we want to be successful at anything we do, we must learn how to work effectively and harmoniously with each other. It can be at the work place, at church, or at a community level. We must learn to tolerate others with their differences.

Jesus chose twelve disciples, each unique in his own way. Thomas was a doubter who never believed anything unless he could perceive it from a humanistic point of view. Peter was easily angered, Judas was a traitor, and the list goes on. But in spite of their differences, they had to learn to work with each other.

I have had the privilege of working with a young lady whose mood for the day can be determined by her greetings in the morning. If, after she says good morning and asks if you have seen her favorite soap opera, then you know she is in a good mood and will be for the rest of the day. But if she greets you with a lousy good morning and does not ask about the soap opera, then you know you should not talk to her for the rest of the day. In spite of her personality, we got along very well. She was understood.

I also have worked with others who would go out of their way to make sure your life is miserable. They are never satisfied with your performance. They put you down and make your life at work a living hell. And still, I have worked with others who want nothing but the best for you and would work with you to ensure the success of a common objective. Working with people like this helps to boost your self-confidence and effectiveness and provide motivation to be the best you can ever be.

Working as a grade coordinator at Anchovy High School, I have had the opportunity to work with the best and most cooperative set of teachers. They tried their best to enhance present effective programs and assisted with the implementation of new programs. Not many coordinators were that fortunate. These teachers taught me that, "Cooperation coupled with zeal can accomplish what zeal alone cannot do."

In working with people, you will have to appreciate them for who they are. You will have to accept the negatives as well as the positives. No one is perfect. We all have our shortcomings and, just as you want them to accept you, you must accept them, too. Be interested in their interests. People often become irritated and aggressive when their interests are ignored. Listen to their point of view and respect them for even making a contribution, no matter how small it may be.

I admired this couple who were my friends back home in Jamaica. As long as what the husband was about to do made him happy, his wife supported him the best way possible. In other words, she put his happiness above her own.

At Bullock Heights Youth Club when I was president, we would never pursue a goal unless there was common consensus. That was the only way to ensure cooperation. We would listen to each other's point of view and agree on a specific course of action. If spouses would learn to do the same thing then there would be more unity in the family. But when the husband, for example, says it is my way or no way, there can be no unity.

Likewise, parents need to listen to their children. They too have minds of their own and can help in decision-making. Doing this will help them develop a sense of responsibility, and when things do not go as planned everyone shares the failure.

Don't hesitate to commend others when they have done well. Give a word of encouragement when it is least expected. If you are afraid to verbalize it, write a note. Never forget that encouragement sweetens labor. Even if the job done wasn't as good as you expected it to be, find something good to commend the person for, even if only for the effort. Then with gentleness, point out the areas where improvement is needed.

Trust and commitment are essential ingredients to the development of good-working relationships. If any are violated, the relationship will never be the same. The more trustworthy and committed you are, the better will be your relationship with others. You will prove to be a person of your word. However, if after you have made a promise and for some reason or another you are unable to fulfill the promise, make sure to explain why it could not be kept. Do not make promises you know you cannot keep.

Paul admonished us in Ephesians 4:32, "Be ye kind one to another, tender-hearted, forgiving one another, even as God for Christ sake hath forgiven you." Stephen Covey said in his book *The Seven Habits of Effective People*, "Little kindness and courtesies are so important. Small discourtesies, little unkindnesses, little forms of disrespect make large withdrawals. In relationships, little things are the big things." So be as courteous and respectful as you can. This will pay great dividends.

For you to be served, you have to first serve others. A former supervisor demonstrated this principle when he picked up his mop and wiped the floor as any of us would do. He never commanded us to do it. And as a result, he was given great respect. Our relationship was such that, even when our task became a little unbearable, we could muster the courage and devote the time and technique needed to get it done. And together we shared the reward. How could production not be boosted?

When you love others with unconditional love, with no strings attached, you are giving them the opportunity to be themselves, to feel secure and safe, and to grow naturally. They will be better able to cooperate with others, to contribute more to society, to develop self-confidence, and to create the best working relationship you will ever experience.

Chapter Nineteen

Living in the Now

I know how to live on almost nothing or with everything. I have learned the secret of living in every situation, whether it is with a full stomach or empty, with plenty or little.

Philippians 4:12

Depression is a killer, and becoming anxious about the future sometimes leads us into the path of this great killer. Men are afraid that when they hit their mid-fifties, they may not be able to function sexually and may lose their spouse as a result. Women are afraid of their menopausal years due to the content of the package. Teenagers fear adulthood and think they may end up with the wrong partners in life. Employees are fearful that tomorrow they may be out of a job, and, on the other hand, employers are fearful that their companies may not be able to withstand the challenges of a competitive market. Parents are fearful that they may not have their children around for long, and the world in general is afraid of global warming, terrorist attacks, and the end of time. But, Philippians 4:12 (NLT) says, "I know how to live on almost nothing or with everything; I have learned the secret of living in every situation, whether it is with a full stomach or empty, with plenty or with little."

When you learn to live in the now, to be contented where you are right now, to accept the things you have no control over, and to see every situation as an opportunity, you will experience a peace that passes all understanding. You will find it in your heart to forgive those who have wronged you. You will say, "Yes, Lord, though I am late for my appointment, thank you for the delay." You will not be a victim of depression but rather one who has learned to say, "Thank you, Lord. Though I don't know why you've allowed it to happen, I know that you know what is best for me and so I trust you to work through me and for me."

When you trust God with your life, He will direct your every step. So when things are not going your way, let go and let God. When the Valentine's date does not turn up, don't cry and feel sorrow for yourself. Give thanks to God; He may just be proving to you one more time that you have made the wrong choice. And you know what? God has the right person for you. Trust Him to manifest that person in your life.

Worrying about the future is a waste of time and is not good. All it does is allow you to be anxious for nothing. The wise King Solomon said in Ecclesiastes 2:18-19, "I came to hate all hard work here on earth, for I must leave to others everything I have earned. And who can tell whether my successors will be wise or foolish? Yet they will control everything I have gained by my skill and hard work under the sun. How meaningless."

So don't be like those who worry about storage for the future, trust God to take you through, for He knows exactly what will happen. I am not saying that you are not to prepare for Mr. Rainy Day, but don't become too anxious as you do not know what tomorrow holds for you.

Let Tomorrow Be Tomorrow

It is silly of us to have the weight of today and then add tomorrow's weight to it. No wonder sometimes we become hypertensive; no wonder cardiovascular diseases are among the leading killers in our nation. Much of the illnesses that we are faced with today are a result of taking on unnecessary worries of tomorrow. And many times our worries are no worries at all. It is our perception of our situation that creates the problems. But if you will learn to look at things from God's perspective, if you will learn to take God at His words, then you will realize that there is really nothing to worry about.

Who told you that the dream you have had for many years now will not be realized? Who told you that because you are getting up in age, you will not find a partner? Who told you that the house you longed to own will not be yours? Trust God to work through you and for you.

Every single day comes with its own package, and sometimes what you are looking for just has not come. But since life goes on, whatever you are handed, give God thanks. If the content is pain and misery, tell yourself that that too will pass. Nothing under the sun lasts forever. Again, King Solomon reminds us in Ecclesiastes 3:1-3 that, "To everything there is a season, and a time for every purpose under the heaven: A time to be born, and a time to die; a time to plant and a time to pluck up that which is planted; a time to kill, and a time to heal; a time to break down and a time to build up."

Tomorrow never comes. You can't live for tomorrow. Every day you must live for today. You do not have the power to cancel today for tomorrow, for every tomorrow becomes a today and each time you get closer to tomorrow, it evades you and presents you with another today. So no wonder the scripture says, "Now is the appointed time." You are sure of the now in today, but you are not sure of the now in tomorrow. Why? Because there is no now in tomorrow.

It is wise to make plans for the future but it should not be such that you work yourself to death today with the hope of enjoying tomorrow. The truth is there may never be a tomorrow. Make your plans with an attitude that says, "Nevertheless Lord, not my will but thine be done." Live life one day at a time, like the song says:

> One day at a time, sweet Jesus,
> That's all I'm asking of you,
> Just give me the strength to do every day
> What I have to do,
> Yesterday's gone, sweet Jesus
> And tomorrow may never be mine,
> Lord, for my sake, teach me to take
> One day at a time.

No matter what situation you are in today, there is a purpose for that situation, and it does not categorize you as good or bad. A meaningful situation may have brought you there. It may have been a result of a decision you made. At the time you thought you were making the right decision, though later it appears to have been the wrong decision. But to God, it may not be wrong since that's the only way to learn the lesson He wants you to learn. Again, my purpose for coming to the United States was meaningful, though at present I wish things were otherwise. But God knows all things best, and, as a Christian, I know that love is the motivating factor for God doing anything in my life.

One of the problems for us not being able to let tomorrow be tomorrow is our lack of faith. We find it difficult to trust God with tomorrow. Dr. Wayne Dyer said in his book, *Manifest Your Destiny*, "Learning to trust may be difficult in the beginning. It will be an exercise in futility if you rely upon your mind to create trust. This is because the mind works on material problems by interpreting sensory data. When you turn toward spiritual matters, the mind attempts to come up with intellectual answers by using proofs, logic, and theoretical reasoning. It demands assurance and proof establishes tangible results."

Have you ever been in a situation where you think the worst will happen only to find out that, after all, it was not so bad?

Sometimes the mound is perceived as a mountain, when the truth is it is just a mound. Learn to accept things as they are, and for what you don't understand, trust God to provide you with the wisdom to approach it the best way possible. Let tomorrow be tomorrow and continue living in the now.

Take Small Steps

Before a baby learns to walk properly, he first has to learn to take small steps. Every parent becomes excited when his/her baby takes his/her first step. But with each step, the child becomes better at walking and eventually starts running. The same is true with us. As we progress in life, we have to learn to take small steps. Nothing happens overnight. Only by taking these small steps, living in the now, will we see improvements in the events that constitute our lives.

Whatever we hope to achieve in the future starts in the now. If you hope to be a guitarist in the future, start with small steps by learning the parts of the guitar. If you don't know what a fret is, how can you follow the instructions for holding different notes? If you want to be a psychologist, start with small steps. Every successful person in life starts with small steps. Goal-setting is a small step. You have to know where you want to go and get there by taking small steps. Each time you make these small steps, you will be encouraged to make bigger steps, but don't be discouraged when you fail. Remember that a baby falls many times before he is able to walk properly. The baby never fails. For him, falling is encouragement to try again. If you learn to get up after a fall, then you too will experience the joy of running later on.

You don't have to wait to be struck by a lightning bolt of time winding down to start with your small steps. As long as you know for sure what it is that you hope to achieve, you can start right where you are this minute and take your steps. It may be as simple as putting your ideas on paper. It could be putting a small amount of money into a savings account. It may be taking the time to learn some musical notes; it may be saying *no* to those high-calorie foods that you have been consuming all your life.

Everything in life goes through stages of development. The oak tree starts from a breakdown of an acorn. The baby starts from a fertilized ovum. Becoming a Christian starts from a true confession of one's sins. Hence, whatever you hope to be or to achieve in life you have to first start with small steps.

Some people sit around waiting for the misfortune of another before they decide to start. The child of rich parents sits down and waits for the inheritance from those parents. I once had a student who was told that all his father owned had been willed to him. I noticed that he would sit in class and do nothing. Each time I approached him, he would remind me that he did not have to work as hard as the others for he was already rich. One day I said to him, "Yes, that may be true, but it would be wise of you to learn all you can so you will know how to maintain your riches. For if you don't know how to do that, you will have it today and lose it tomorrow."

With each small step you take, there are valuable lessons to learn. You will learn what to do and what not to do; who to trust and who not to trust. You will be given the wisdom and the assurance for the next step. You will learn that with God nothing is impossible. Your foundation will be strong and firm.

The man who suddenly reaches the top in life usually never knows how to manage himself up there. He often looks down with fear of losing his balance. As a result, he will hang on as though his life depends totally on it. People in this category do not know the beauty of giving to the poor and needy, as they think that the more they give the less wealth they'll have, but it is indeed the opposite. The more you give the more you receive.

Learning to take small steps is not baby-like. It is maturity. The baby who has just been born cannot make small steps until he has reached a level of maturity. So if you think that taking small steps, such as planning your career path, is immature, then you are up for the shock of your life. You are still at the newborn stage.

Take time out to know what you want and go after it. Writing this book started with very small steps. Most of the time when I start a new chapter, I have no idea how to start. But by taking a small step, such as meditation, I am given ideas galore. Once I start writing, I have to force myself to stop!

Be Great Now

Greatness doesn't necessarily means doing great things. Sometimes it means doing the little things that allow you to move towards living a fulfilled life. Not everyone was created to be a teacher, not everyone a doctor or the prime minister or the president of a country. To be great now is to follow that still, small voice within and to walk in the wisdom that is God given.

By now you should learn how to go after your dreams, how to discover your purpose in this life, how to understand yourself better, and be encouraged to get up from your comfort zone and be the best you can ever be.

Be happy about who you are and what you do. Allow the love of God to flow in your heart and help you be the person He designed you to be. I realize that the more I ask God to fill my heart with unconditional love, the more I am at peace with myself and the world, and the more I am able to understand the evil influences around me. Having this knowledge allows me to immunize myself against their effects.

Being great now means to cherish the relationship you have with God; to walk hand in hand with him. It means to be so close to Him that you become co-creator with Him. It's a wonderful experience to walk each day with the Lord. The devil is busy working around the clock always seeking ways to defeat you. He gets into your thoughts and causes you to focus on that which is negative about yourself and the situation you may be in. But with God in your life, these thoughts can be quickly dispelled and replaced with more positive and enriching thoughts.

God promised to bless you, but perhaps you have lost a friend you felt was valuable and you begin to wonder how you are going to manage. You begin to think that something must be wrong with you, or your friend would still be with you. But have you ever stopped to think that maybe there is not something is wrong with you, but with your friend? He or she may have missed the opportunity for a good life with you.

Follow the path God is putting you on. Go where he wants you to go. Be like Abraham and don't question God why you should go, for the truth is, He will lead you only in the path of greatness. You may feel discouraged and downhearted, but don't give up. God is with you.

I thought of going back home to Jamaica because I longed to see my children. God knew my heart was fixated on going home and, after praying about it and looking for God's direction, He sent a messenger to me one morning as I waited in church. I had never seen this man in my life. He was a total stranger and, as a matter of fact, I have not seen him since.

God sent me the answers to the questions I had asked him. It was amazing! I have never had anyone tell me things that were puzzling me before. But God works in mysterious ways and sometimes the way you want him to answer your prayer, is not the way He chooses to answer it. That's why it is important to let go and let God.

To be great, God will supply you with the wisdom, knowledge, and understanding you need. You will find yourself doing things that you never thought you would be able to do. Others will see the worth within you and marvel.

Give God the glory and the honor due to His name. Rise up from where you are right now and take the small steps towards greatness, which is found only in Jesus Christ.

Chapter Twenty

Living without Attachment

Yes everything else is worthless when compared with the Infinite value of knowing Christ Jesus my Lord. For his sake I have discarded everything else, counting it all garbage so that I could gain Christ and become one with him. I no longer count on my own righteousness through obeying the law, but rather, I become righteous through faith in Christ.

Philippians 3:8-9, NLT

Every family carries its own traditions, and it is natural for us to feel attached to these traditions. In my family, for example, three quarters of my relatives worship on a Saturday, as that was the worship day for my grandparents. The other quarter worships on Sunday. My father was the one to actually break the tradition by choosing to worship on Sunday. As children growing up, my parents made it compulsory for us to go to church unless we were sick and could not walk, even if it meant that we went and returned home after.

Another tradition was that we could not go to sleep at night without first reading our Bible and praying. If we were to fall asleep without doing either, we would be awakened from our sleep. Sometimes at this point we couldn't even see the words in the Bible clearly, as there was still some sleep in our eyes. After that we were to pray and say goodnight to everyone in order of seniority. If Angella prayed she would say, "Goodnight Papa, goodnight Mama, goodnight Sister Maizie," and down the line it went. It was fun, though, to have to wake up Angella, as she would do quite the opposite of what she was asked to do.

Everyone has some form of attachment, whether it is tradition, the past, people, finances, successes, or failures. But living with attachment sometimes robs us of who we are, the purpose for which we were created: joy and happiness. Oftentimes our attachment to tradition is so powerful that if we decide to become detached, we are alienated from friends, family, and neighbors. Tradition sometimes dictates who our friends should be, who we should marry, the course of study we should pursue, what to listen to, and how we should speak. If we choose to do otherwise, we are often seen as the black sheep of the family and, in the case of a friendship, a traitor.

Something as simple as a voting decision that is cohesive to the traditions of the family can cause alienation or death. You may never be allowed to participate in any family activities and may be seen as the cause of friction in the family. Sometimes when a parent/child relationship is destroyed, a sibling's relationship may be affected, too. So sometimes to avoid these conflicts, you may decide to go along, whether you are in agreement or not. That to me is like living in bondage. Although slavery was abolished in most parts of the world, some of us are still enslaved mentally. The honorable Bob Marley sang, "Emancipate yourself from mental slavery, none but ourselves can free our minds."

Prior to his conversion the Apostle Paul followed traditions to a T. He was zealous in persecuting the Christians. But after his strange encounter with God, he learned to break away from tradition; to detach himself and become engrossed in his new way of living. That is why in Philippians 3:8-9 he confidently says, "Yes, everything else is worthless when compared with the infinite value of knowing Christ Jesus, my Lord. For his sake, I have discarded everything else, counting it all garbage so that I could gain Christ and become one with him. I no longer count on my own righteousness through the faith in Christ." Following traditions is sometimes not the best thing to do.

We sometimes become so attached to the past that we produce stagnancy or death in all areas of our lives. Sometimes we are so attached that to move forward brings us pain. I was associated with a young man who had become so attached to his past that he was afraid to move forward. He could frequently be heard saying things like, "If I were still at— then I would be better off." I am not saying the past is not important, but rather that you should not become so attached to it that you become afraid of moving forward.

The more we have, the more we want, and the more wealth we acquire, the more we become attached. The banking sector has become so unstable and insecure that someone said it is better to put your money under your mattress. But even there it is not safe, since you can lose it through fire or theft. Attachment to possessions breeds insecurity. You may walk the street looking over your shoulder for one who may want to steal from you.

I heard the story of a man who went to the bank to withdraw some money. He came out of the bank, went to the taxi stand, and waited for a cab when a pickpocket walked up to him and demanded the money he had just withdrawn. Feeling helpless, he handed over all he had to the thief. After the realization hit the man that he had no money left to pay the cab driver, he said to the thief, "Imagine, you haven't even left me with taxi fare!" The thief responded by giving him the fare and then said to him, "Man, do you know that I am working?" He then fled.

Hanging on to your success does not make any sense at all. This produces fear of failure, and it is through failure that we learn. I have not yet met a successful person who has not experienced some level of failure in his/her life.

Attachment to other people is another problem you may be faced with. You can be so attached to your children that you provide no room for their development. You can be so attached to your spouse you think life is meaningless without him/her. You can be so attached to your friend that providing them space, gives rise to jealousy.

Detaching yourself from people will give them the chance to make decisions on their own and to make choices that are more consistent to the way they think. You will find that your level of self-confidence will not be threatened by what others think of you.

Detaching yourself from sicknesses will bring you healing that you never thought possible. A miracle will only happen when you have learned to detach yourself. Pray about it and leave it there.

You can only experience growth if you learn to detach yourself from possessions, people, traditions, sickness, or ideas. That's the only time you will experience happiness and peace of mind. The more attached you are, the more insecure and unhappy you will be.

For you to be all that God wants you to be, you have to detach yourself from everything. At this point, you have given God the chance to work through you and for you. You will experience the flow of spiritual energy that is needed to sustain you and bring you to the place that you want to be. Detachment allows you to move with the flow of that which you have no control. So if your spouse asks you for a divorce, don't think that it is the end of the world, instead it may be the beginning of a new life—sometimes a better one. Live without attachment and experience the blessings of the Lord upon your life.

What You Have Is a Gift

We bring nothing into this world and we will take nothing out. Everything that we have is a gift from God. Our successes, our friends, our finances, our families, our neighbors—all of these and more are gifts. When we die, nothing that we have achieved can be taken with us, although family and friends may attempt to put them in our caskets, of what use will they be to us? Absolutely none!

What you have today is given to you as gifts. They were given to you to help make your life a little brighter and to enhance the kingdom of God. The wise King Solomon in Ecclesiastes 5:18-19 said, "Even so, I have noticed one thing at least, that is good. It is so good for people to eat, drink, and enjoy their work under the sun during the short life God has given them, and to accept their lot in life. And it is a good thing to receive wealth from God and the good health to enjoy it. To enjoy your work and accept your lot in life- this is indeed a gift from God."

Though you may have worked hard to achieve all you have, it is still a gift. Today you may have it and tomorrow it may be gone. I have often come across people who were really living it up, forgetting the one who gave them the gifts they were using. But in the twinkle of an eye, all they had was lost. This reminds me of the earthquake in Haiti in 2010. I was in the process of writing this book when it happened. Thousands of people lost their lives and millions were left homeless. Children became orphans. The rich, the poor, the middle-class—everyone in that region was affected. Mother Nature did not destroy the poor and leave the rich, or vice-versa—every man, woman, and child was affected.

Life is a gift and should not be taken for granted. Each day we need to give God thanks and to remember that the world belongs to him and not to us. I love the words of this song:

There are things that I love,
And hold dear to my heart,
They're just borrowed,
They are not mine at all.
Jesus only let me use them
To brighten my life,
So remind me,
Oh remind me dear Lord.

Sometimes God has to remind us that all we have is His; consequently, failure and losses are memos used to remind us of this fact.

It must have brought God much pain to see our misuse of the resources that he lent us. Instead of using what we have to enhance his kingdom, we use it to glorify the devil. Instead of helping those who are in need, we use what we have for our selfish reasons. We sometimes give to those we know can give back to us.

Use what you have to enhance your life and the lives of others. Being selfish does not pay. There is no blessing to receive from selfishness. Detach yourself from the loan you are given and watch the blessings of God upon your life.

We are all interconnected. What I have is yours and what you have is mine. In our land we pay taxes, which go to benefit us all in the way of better roads, better schools, better utility services, and protection from terrorist attacks. And do you know what? If we could accept the fact that we are interconnected, then resources would not have to be wasted on protecting us from terrorists.

Give God thanks for what you have achieved and do not make the mistake of looking on yourself as the *Great I Am,* for you are not. For all the things that you have acquired—the fresh air you breathe, your friends, and family—all of these are gifts and should not be called otherwise. Just be grateful for what you have and enjoy it all as much as you can.

I can recall the joy of a seven-year-old boy who was rescued after being under rubble for about eight days during the rescue period in Haiti. He lifted his hands towards heaven as though he was saying, "Thank you, God, for sparing my life. Hurray!" Life is the most valuable gift from God, for where there is life, there is hope.

Don't forget to honor God in all you do and say. Thank Him when it is plentiful; thank Him when there is just a little; thank Him in good times and in bad times; thank Him for your failures and your successes; thank Him for all you have. Detach yourself from your earthly treasures and build for yourself treasures in heaven, which have more value.

Ownership of anything in this life is impossible. The God of the universe owns everything. So stop holding on to what is not yours. Simply enjoy them now while you can, for soon you may have them no more.

Give to Receive

As children growing up, many stories were told to us that we actually believed. One such story was about a man in my community who had a big bump in his forehead. The story went that the bump was because he gave something and then took it back. As a result, we were fearful of giving anything before we were sure that that is what we really wanted to do. Eventually, as we got older, we realized that the story was not true; that it was used by our older siblings to manipulate us.

There is joy in giving, and we should not have to be manipulated in any way to give. It should come freely from the heart.

In Mark 10:17-22, we learn that as Jesus started out on a journey to Jerusalem, a rich man ran and knelt down before him, and asked what he must do to be saved. Jesus quoted part of the Ten Commandments to the man. The man's response was, "Master, I've obeyed all these commandments since I was young." Jesus looked at the man with genuine love and said to him, "There is still one thing that you haven't done. Go sell all your possessions and give the money to the poor, and you will have treasure in heaven. Then come and follow me." The rich man thought that was a hard thing to do, so he left sorrowfully.

Further in the chapter, Jesus said that everyone who has given up a house, or brothers or sisters or mother or father or children or property for His sake and for the good news, would receive in return a hundred times as many houses, brothers, sisters, mothers, children, and property, along with persecution. And in the world to come that person would have eternal life.

Only when you learn to give, will you receive. And the more you give, the more you will receive. In my personal life, I have come to understand that the more I give, the more I receive. The more I detach myself from my possessions, the more I am blessed.

Giving does not necessarily mean giving money. You are rich in resources: time, talent, skills, a listening ear, a smile, or a helping hand. When I was a child and it was time to plant renta yam or guango peas, my father would go and help his friends plant and in turn they would come and give him a hand when his time came around. In other words, one hand washed another. These were usually happy moments for us as children as we too had our part to play. The best part of it was to partake of the food that was prepared.

The more love you give, the more love you receive. And this is true for any relationship whether it be parent/child, spouse, religious, or just simple social relationships. If you want to be loved, find somebody to love. That may be the reason for the love received by Mother Teresa who gave her all to take care of the poor and needy.

Giving grudgingly does little for you. Giving must be done sincerely from the heart and you should not give to show off or to receive anything in return. Many times that is the case with giving: you give only because you know there is a reward to get back. In the United States, people often give to charity to get a tax write-off, but if a poor man turns up at their gates seeking food or clothing, he is turned away because he has nothing to give back or so they think. Just saying, "Thank you and God bless you," brings you unexpected blessings.

Jesus instructed us in Matthew 6:1-4 (NLT) to

> "Watch out! Don't do your good deeds publicly to be admired by others, for you will lose the reward from your

> Father in heaven. When you give to someone in need, don't do as the hypocrites do—blowing your trumpets in the synagogues and streets to call attention to their acts of charity! I tell you the truth; they have received all the rewards they will ever get. But when you give to someone in need, do not let your left hand know what your right hand is doing. Give your gifts in private, and your Father, who sees everything will reward you."

The more attention parents give to their children, the more they will get from them. Today we are often too busy getting on with our private lives that we fail to spend valuable time with our children. No longer do we spend time together. And as a result, relationships are destroyed and we end up with unrest and chaos in our society. Drug abuse and other addictions take root in our children. They grow up not knowing who they are, fighting to find their rightful place in society. Our girls become promiscuous and our boys become restless and irresponsible. We need to help our children develop positive attitudes towards God, towards themselves, towards others, and towards society in general.

I remember a thirteen-year-old boy who attempted suicide twice as a result of failed parental love and guidance. There was no father around and his mother was too busy trying to make ends meet. Our children need us. Let us give them the courage, the strength, the wisdom, and understanding they need to grow into worthwhile men and women.

How much are you giving to God? Are you so busy that you don't remember him until you are helpless? How much of your money are you giving to him? Are you using your talents and abilities to enhance his kingdom or are you using them to promote evil in our society? Remember that you will be held accountable for all that he has entrusted in your care.

Detach yourself from the material things of this life. Don't be so attached that you can't help the poor and needy around you. Don't be so attached that you forget who you are and the purpose for which you were created. I end with the words of Judson W. Van DeVenter's 1896 song:

All to Jesus, I surrender,
All to him I freely give
I will ever love and trust him,
In his presence daily live.
I surrender all,
I surrender all
All to thee, my blessed Savior,
I surrender all.

Stagnant Blessings

If you have a plant that is not getting enough sunshine and water, after a while it will start to wither and eventually die. The beauty once emitted from that plant is no longer appreciated and, oh, what a loss.

When Jesus came upon the fig tree and realized there was no fruit for him to eat, He cursed the tree, and it withered away. Likewise when our lives become a burden and we experience failures and hurts on every side, sometimes it's a result of stagnant blessings. It may be the fruit we reaped from the seeds we sowed. The saying goes, what goes around comes around. "Be not deceived. God is not mocked. Whatsoever a man soweth that shall he also reap."

You can experience whatever blessing you want to in life, but you will have to be careful with the seeds you sow. For instance, you will not get love if you don't give love; you will not be helped in times of need if you do not help others when they seek your help in times of need. If you lie and cheat your way in life, the day will come when you will realize that it was useless. You will lose everything you have acquired during that time of lying and cheating. The same way you seek to use, abuse, and manipulate others, is the same way you will be used, abused, and manipulated. Don't think for one moment that you will escape, because you won't. It may not be by the people you abused, but by others. So be careful of the seeds you sow.

Life is so meticulous that sometimes what we do will not affect us, but will affect our children and grandchildren. That's referred to as a generational curse. Life takes note of everything we do. Nothing goes unnoticed. That is why we are encouraged not to render evil for evil. but instead do what is right in the eyes of God. If you sow good seeds, you will start to see God's blessings in your life.

If you are not experiencing any growth in your life, you need to take an inventory to see where the blockage is. Sometimes you may have to make an adjustment in your attitude towards God, towards yourself, and towards others. Sometimes you have to check the fertilizer you were given. Is it one that will promote growth or retard growth? Seeds of selfishness, greed, or pride will not bring you growth. These seeds will never thrive, even if they are sown on good soil. When you look out only for your needs and not for the needs of others, you are stifling your own growth. We are all connected and depend on each other for survival, so it pays to treat others as you would like them to treat you.

I remember in primary school, when cheating was forbidden, if we could help a friend, we would. Unfortunately, we had a friend who was quick to show you the answers to a problem, or so we thought. But her anxiety was a result of supplying the wrong answers! After showing you, she would erase all her wrong answers and write the correct ones. That to me was a high level of selfishness and dishonesty. Nothing happens in life without proper records and, though you may think that nobody will find out, God sees you and takes note of it. So be careful!

The scripture says that lying lips are an abomination to the Lord and will hinder the blessings from flowing in your life. Ananias and Sapphira in Acts Chapter 5 thought they could lie in order to keep what was not theirs. But oh no! They could not, and did not get away with it. They were both killed. Lying lips will kill relationships by destroying confidence and trust. When spouses start to lie to each other, the blessing they used to enjoy will be taken away. Lying is one of the reasons for so many broken relationships in our society today. I remember a gem I learned at primary school that says, "Speak the truth and speak it ever, Cause it what it will, He who hides the wrong he did, Does the wrong things still."

If you learn to love others unconditionally, you will experience the flow of God's blessings in your life. God is love and there is no way God can abide in your heart if you do not have love. Once malice, hatred, and strife infest your mind, the flow of God's rich blessings will be blocked. But the truth is, it will be cleared when you take control and replace negative thoughts and emotions with positive ones.

Sometimes your blessings become stagnant because you left everything to God and you did nothing. John Gray writes in his book, *How to Get What You want And Have What You Want*, "For God's blessings to take hold in our lives, we must do everything within our power to get what we need. We cannot expect God to do it all. It does not work that way. God only takes the parts that we can't do." So if you want to experience blessings in your life, start moving. Start doing what you know you are supposed to do. Then you will experience inner and outer success and can look back on all that you have been through and learn from it and meet the other challenges you are likely to face. Life is full of challenges no matter how successful you are. Let the love of God flow in your heart and give you victory over stagnant blessings.

Chapter Twenty-one

On Your Way through Life

By faith Abraham, when he was called to go out into a place which he should after receive for an inheritance, obeyed, and he went out, not knowing whither he went.

Hebrews 11:8

There should be no doubt in your mind that life is indeed a journey and for every new experience there come new trials, temptations, and decisions as to whether you will win or lose. Do you adapt the principles of inhabitants or do you set your own standards with a winning attitude? Do you continue to walk by faith or do you become fearful when you meet the giants?

The children of Israel were on their journey to the Promised Land and as soon as they won a battle and hoped to relax, there came another battle. They almost gave up when the spies came back to tell them there were great giants in the land. But they had the assurance that, though there were many giants, the victory was already theirs through God.

You were not promised sunshine all the time. There will be nights, too. You were not promised a well-paved road, but one that has potholes, too.

Coming to the United States of America, I thought that everything would be all right. No more would I have to walk off the tips of my shoes as I did in Jamaica. I came to a rude awakening when I realized that potholes were here, too and also flooding in some areas when it rained! I thought it was only in Santa Cruz and Montego Bay, Jamaica that these things happened!

Every step you take in life will bring its own heartaches, joy, sorrow, and pain, but no matter what stage you are in, there are numerous lessons to be learned. What you make of these experiences and lessons will help to determine whether you become a victim or a victor. It is hoped that at the end of this chapter you will refuse to live in defeat but instead choose to be victorious in all your battles.

No Mistakes, Just Lessons

Have you ever noticed that the hardest lessons to learn are those that you *must* learn? If your dream is to become a doctor, then chemistry, physics, and biology are subjects that you must master. No matter how hard you have to study, you must be successful in these subjects to pursue your dream. In other words, success comes through hard work. If the first time you sit examinations and fail, you will have to re-sit them or else you will never accomplish your dream as a doctor. It is the same with life, you will not be successful until you have learned the lessons it teaches.

Make no mistake about it, there is no mistake in life. What you call mistakes are simply lessons you must learn and, until they are learned, you will always be in the classroom. The only time you will be promoted is when you have passed the test. Brian Luke Seaward says, "Man is a spirit on a human path." Every experience you encounter, whether good or bad, is a lesson you must learn. That's the only way you can be successful on your human path.

I asked a friend how things were going with him, and his response was, "Challenges, challenges, challenges."

I said to him, "Brother, welcome to life, because that's the only way you know if you are experiencing life and death. No challenge at all signifies death. Which do you prefer life or death?"

Some children born in this life are what others classify as mistakes. Marriages break up because of mistakes, jobs are lost because of mistakes, and Christians give up because of mistakes. But we all need to wake up to the fact that nothing that happens is a mistake. Everything is a lesson for us to learn, and the faster we learn, the better our lives will be. There would be fewer mistaken children, the divorce rate would decrease, jobs would be more secure, Christians would be more dedicated, and overall the world would be a better place to live in once we learn our lessons.

David learned his lesson after he arranged for Potiphar's death in the battlefront. In Psalm 51, he wrote, "Create in me a clean heart and renew a right spirit within me." Saul was a persecutor of Christians but when afflicted with blindness, asked, "Lord what will thou have me do?" He learned his lesson and became a great ambassador for God. AIDS patients would perhaps be the first to encourage you to use a condom before sexual intercourse because they have reaped the reward of sexual mistakes (lessons). The student whose dream is to move on to college but failed his or her exams will have learned that success is the reward for hard work. There are absolutely no mistakes in life, even if your character is damaged. What you call mistakes are structured lessons for you to learn.

When are we going to learn that anything hidden in the closet will be revealed? A friend invited an insurance agent to her house who asked her if she drank any form of alcohol. My friend's response was *no*. But like a touch of bad luck, at that precise moment a bottle of alcohol fell from her top kitchen cupboard!

For you to be a better you today for tomorrow you must see the lesson in every bad experience that you encounter. That's the only way you will be promoted in life's educational system.

When You Are Handed a Lemon

If this is the case, then make lemonade. Inspirational stories are told time and time again of people who have met misfortune in life and have turned such into marvelous opportunities. One such person is a former supervisor who was shot in the back on his farm. As a result, he is crippled and has to move around in wheelchair. But he did not bury himself in the mud of self-pity or defeat; instead, from his wheelchair he preaches the good message of salvation. So when life hands you a lemon, make lemonade.

When I came to the United States, I had just completed a Bachelor of Arts degree in primary education, yet I found myself working a live-in job where I took care of a stroke patient. I have learned that sometimes life takes you on a totally different path from what you had in mind. I never sat down and mourned. Instead, I used my time as best as possible. During times when there wasn't much to do, I read or wrote. From that, came my book.

If you have lost the home that you invested all your savings in, look at what you did wrong so that if you are given the chance again, you will know what to do. See this as an opportunity to reinvest wisely in another home.

Make the best lemonade that anyone will ever drink. In other words, people will be so inspired by your actions that they will always make reference to your school of wisdom. I used to hate when my father came in late at night to ask me to make him a cup of lemonade, but I guess my lemonade used to be so refreshing that he chose not to do it himself.

There are things in life that you will have no control over, but when you receive them, make the best use of them. Before you receive your blessings in life, there has to be a period of preparation, hence, the lemon you are sometimes given is a test to see what you will do with it. So don't sit and squash it, use it to make the best lemonade.

After God's promise came that he would bless me for 2010, I stopped working for one month and got half the salary I was used to getting. One day as I lay on my couch thinking about life and how unfair it is sometimes, a voice said to me, "Maize, get up from where you are and be alive again. Don't you see what I am doing for you? I am preparing you for the blessing I have in store for you. Here I have given you the time to relax at home and to finish your book." Without hesitation, I got up from the chair and went to my computer to continue writing, and in my heart I said, "Thank you God for your blessings." I never fell back into that state again. So when you are handed a lemon, use it to make lemonade.

Which Is Your Choice, a Victim or a Victor?

It is no coincidence that the words victim and victor both have the same first four letters. The words victim and victor have the same root origin. The prefix "vict" comes from Latin and means to conquer. Of course, the victor is the one who does the conquering and the victim is the one who is conquered. I am going to take it that that implies they both share the same circumstances, but the outcomes are different. In other words, you and I can share a similar experience but I choose to be a victor while you choose to be a victim. Depending on your attitude towards the circumstances of your life, you can either be a victim or a victor.

Let's look at this scenario for example: Lady A and Lady B were both diagnosed with breast cancer. Lady A knows that no matter what happens to her or how bad her situation is God will see her through. So she goes along with the treatments prescribed by her doctor and her spirit is always up.

Lady B on the other hand, falls into self-pity and blames everyone for what is happening to her. As a matter of fact, she actually gives up on herself, thinking there is nothing anyone can do. As a result she stops her treatment and sits down, waiting for death. Which of the two would you say is the victim? Of course, without a doubt, it is Lady B.

You cannot allow your circumstances to determine your destiny. You have to rise above them and take control. That's the only way to be a victor. You have lived where you are for over a year and you've never owed your landlord any money, but suddenly you find yourself without a job and now you do owe him. After explaining your situation to the landlord, he chooses not to understand, and instead gives you one month to leave the apartment. Don't be distraught. Don't give up. You have rights, too. But before you attempt to do anything say, "Lord why did you allow this? There may be something you are trying to tell me. Give me the wisdom to understand what you are saying." You might be surprised to know that God is saying it is time to move on and if that is not His will, He will work things out for you. Be a victor.

Now let's take a look at some of the differences between a victim and a victor:

- A victim sees his circumstances as a death sentence and thinks there is no way he can live through it. Meanwhile the victor acts like Job and says, "Though he slay me, yet will I serve him." Though my situation may be painful, but I know that it too will pass.
- The victim says, "Why me?" The victor says, "I know I have been chosen to go through this and I will come forth as pure gold."
- The victim says, "I am a loser." The victor says, "Though I may be labeled a loser, I am determined to be all that God intended me to be. I am going to show the world how great and valuable I am."
- The victim says, "I will never make it." The victor says, "I can do all things through Christ which strengthened me."
- The victim says, "I am fearful that things will never be the same." The victor says, "Though I walk

> through the valley of the shadow of death I will fear no evil for thou art with me. Thy rod and thy staff they comfort me."

Decide today whether to be a victor or a victim. Refuse to succumb. No matter how rough the road may be, continue to walk, as you are not alone. God promised to be there for you and He will be. Nothing that happens to you happened by chance. It happened for a reason. So be a victor and not a victim. I end this chapter with a quote by Gail Brook Burket:

> I do not ask to walk smooth paths
> Nor bear an easy load.
> I pray for strength and fortitude
> To climb the rock-strewn road.
> Give me such courage and
> I can scale the hardest peaks alone,
> And transform every stumbling block
> Into a stepping stone.

Chapter Twenty-two

Living a Satisfied Life

I have fought the good fight, I have finished the race, and I have remained faithful.

2 Timothy 4:7

Man is never satisfied. He has an insatiable appetite. There is always the longing for more, and the more he has, the more he wants. Though he may achieve all that he hopes to achieve, he is still not satisfied and, as long as he lives, he may never be satisfied. So the question is, Is there hope that man can live a satisfied life? Can he experience real fulfillment? My answer to these questions is "yes."

As I have discussed before, everyone was created for a purpose. God did not idly create you. In order to experience a satisfied life, you have to discover the purpose for which you were created and have it fulfilled in alignment with the word of God. Once you walk the path He designed for you, you will be endowed with peace, joy, love, contentment, and happiness. Though you may have to cross rivers and climb mountains, you will be inundated with blessings from above. You will look back and wonder how you made it. How did you reach where you are? Then you'll acknowledge that it was not you, but the Christ that lives in you. The bottom line is that only He can bring you the satisfaction of living a satisfied life.

When you allow God to be the shepherd of your life, He will lead you in the path you must go. If the children of Israel had obeyed God, their journey to the Promised Land would not have taken so long. Moses did not see the Promised Land because of his disobedience. God instructed him to speak to the rock, but instead, he struck it. This was a sign of poor attitude, disobedience, and egoism. It is our human nature to think that we know more than God or that He is incapable of leading us on the path.

All the topics I have dealt with so far in this book are aimed at helping you live a satisfied life. If we allow love to guide us in our choices and everyday activities, we will be on the path towards a satisfied life.

Our days in this life are numbered. No one knows for sure how long he/she has, and that is why there is this urgency to do what we can now, today, as we may not be privileged to have tomorrow. As I have said before, opportunity comes but once. Miss it today and you may not get it back tomorrow.

Walk with a humble heart, as God hates a proud spirit. Don't think of yourself more highly than you ought to think. Accept others as part of you. And as a matter of fact, that's exactly what they are. We are all connected. What happens in one part of this world affects the other parts. The world has become a globalized community. When God asked Cain for his brother, Cain answered, "Am I my brother's keeper?" The truth is Cain did not realize that in destroying Abel, he was destroying a part of himself.

Commit your ways to the Lord and let Him continue to direct your steps. Don't make decisions on your own without talking to God about it. Let Him know that you acknowledge Him as the master of your life. Give him your spouse, your children, your business, your finances—give him your all—and let him lead you into a satisfied life. At the end of the day you can say like the writer of 2 Tim 4:7, "I have fought a good fight, I have finished the race, and I have remained faithful."

Living in Contentment

It pays to serve Jesus.
I speak from my heart,
For he is always with us,
If we do our part.
There is naught in this wide world,
Can pleasure afford?
There is peace and contentment
In serving the Lord.

When you are down and out and think there is nothing to look forward to in this life, commit your all to God. Tell Him all that you are experiencing. Though He knows, He wants you to acknowledge Him. He wants you to make your own choice of asking for His help or not. I find great pleasure in talking to Him about everything in my life even though it may be trivial. But He is my best friend. When there is no one else around to talk to, I talk to Him. He is a good listener. Sometimes He assures me, "Maizie, don't worry. I am working on it for you." And with this comes tremendous peace and contentment.

Don't envy your neighbor for what he/she has, or you will never be content. Your neighbor drives a Mercedes Benz, but this does not mean that you have to drive one, too. Be satisfied with the car you have as long as it takes you where you want to go.

Don't borrow money unnecessarily in order to build a home like your neighbor. Wait until you can afford to have what you want. Maybe your neighbor wishes he/she had more discipline where spending is concerned. Many times the load that we carry is of our own making. We never learn to be satisfied.

Don't be dissatisfied with your present situation and long to return to the past, for it will never happen. The past is the past. Look ahead of you, not behind. Lot's wife became a pillar of salt because she looked back with a longing. Don't be a pillar of salt in your present situation. It makes no sense to say if only you could wind back the hands of time, for you can't. Be content where you are until your change comes.

One of the reasons for our dissatisfaction is our inability to wait on our change of season, just like when we can't wait for spring to come. I personally don't like the winter, especially when there are a lot of snowstorms. Your springtime will soon be here and no matter how you try to speed it up, it will never happen before its time.

One thing I know for sure is that nothing happens before its time. If you try to run ahead of time, you will end up feeling more disappointed and frustrated. The chicken will have to wait until the right time before it is hatched. The butterfly if it leaves its cocoon before its time may have problems flying.

If all you have is a quarter, give God thanks and be content, as there is always somebody who is worse than you are. I heard the story of a man who thought that all was lost for him. He had a finger of ripe bananas, took it, and went up in a tree with the hope of hanging himself after he had eaten it. But as he peeled the banana and threw the skin down, he noticed somebody took it up and made a feast of it. He then realized that his situation was not the worst, that there was actually somebody who was worse off than he. He then climbed down from the tree. So, when you think you have come to the end of the road, that there is no hope for you, don't give up. Life goes on. All you may see is despair, but when you think not, then hope brings you peace and contentment and the assurance that you are not alone. God is with you and will be with you to the end of the journey.

Fear Not the Monster Death

David says in Psalm 23:4, "Though I walk through the valley of the shadow of death, I will fear no evil for thou art with me. Thy rod and thy staff they comfort me." No one wants to die. We all wish that we could live on and on and on. But the scripture says, "If it were in this life we have hope we would be men most miserable."

Technology and advanced studies in medicine have paved the path to create youthfulness, even in those who were once young. Plastic surgery now seems to be of great necessity especially to those who can afford it. But so far, no one has been able to add one day to the time when he/she should leave this earth. No matter the amount of plastic surgery, man has an appointment with death and it is not one that can be changed at his convenience. It is sure and it must come. The time you do not know, but it must come. Since it is a sure thing, why do we all fear it? Why can't we simply accept the fact and appreciate it when it comes? Why do we wish it never came? Death has a twinge of finality. It signals the end of life and leaves loneliness and separation among those who are still alive. But here I am telling you not to fear the monster death.

Death is not the end. Death is a transition from one life to another. Every change that we experience in life goes through a period of death. To break the habit of alcoholism, you put to death this habit, to live a life free from alcohol and its addiction; to change your career path you put to death your present career; to walk the Christian pathway, you put to death your former way of life. "Old things are passed away and behold all things have become new." So death should not be feared. It is a transition.

The problem, however, is that the life you live here on earth will determine the life you live after death. Christ promised you eternal life, which means that after your life on earth you will live and reign with him. Otherwise, you will live in eternal punishment. Though different religions have their own concept of life after death, the truth is, it should not be feared. You have the choice of how you want to spend this life after death. Do you want to reign with Christ or do you want to spend your time in hell? In this life there is much confusion, pain, hatred, anger, and strife. I certainly do not want to continue my time in hell! How about you?

Death signals a new beginning. It is the time when you will say good-bye to friends and family to live the life that is awaiting you. I remember my mother's death, how she sang, prayed, and read the scriptures moments before she left this earth. She seemed to have gotten a glimpse of heaven when those at her bedside heard her exclaim, "Oh, the flowers are beautiful. They are all white!" There was a level of excitement in her voice. And in the end, she closed her eyes and took her final breath. It left us lonely and sad, but we are assured of the fact that we will see her again.

Let us not waste our time wishing life to pass. But let us spend our time doing that which we were called to do in this life. Let us treat our brothers and sisters the way we want to be treated. Let us love one another the way we want to be loved. Let us build a little heaven down here and make Christ the center of our lives. Give Him the fear that you may be experiencing right now. Allow Him to guide your life and to give you the peace and contentment you need to live a satisfied life.

A God Realized Life—a Better Life

The aim of this book is to help you create the life that will make you a better you today to go through tomorrow. But it can only be achieved through your acknowledgement that a life without God is no life at all. For all the topics I have discussed, if God is not in the picture, you may never be successful in making you a better you.

If your thoughts are not centered on God, if they are not God-oriented, if they are not positive, then you will continue to live in negativity and will not experience the growth or the change you are hoping for.

What you say is what you get. If you do not speak kind words to others, speak words of wisdom, speak positively, speak as God would have you speak, you may not experience a better you.

Dreams were meant to enhance your life and those of others. God can help you reach for those dreams and be the best that you can ever be.

Don't sit back and think that you can't do it for you can. With God all things are possible. There is no height that you can't reach if you allow him to work through you.

Make use of all the opportunities that come on your path. They come but once. God will send these opportunities to you. He will open doors that you once thought impossible. What he opens stays open until He chooses to close it again.

Exercise faith in Him for without faith it is impossible to please Him. We walk by faith and not by sight.

Discover who you are. Love yourself for who you are. Don't try to change who you are to be accepted by the crowd. For you are just as important as anyone else.

Use your God-given abilities. That's what God expects of you. Don't hide these abilities under a coverall. Be all that you can ever be.

And don't forget that to be inferior is your choice. No one can make you think less of yourself unless you give him or her the opportunity. Change what you can change and accept that which you can't. Ask God for the wisdom to know the difference.

Believe in the God who believes in you and develop an intimate relationship with Him. Give Him the chance to lead you in the path that He knows is best for you.

And in everything, give thanks. Thank Him when things are good. Thank Him when things are bad. Thank Him in the morning, at noon, and in the evening. Thank Him all the time. He allows everything in your life for a reason.

Don't go around blaming others for the mishaps in your life. Look into yourself and claim the blessings that God has in store for you. Claim your finances, your health, your family, and your success.

Don't murmur when things are not going your way for it is all a part of God's will. He is in control. Let Him be the roadmap to your happiness.

Take very good care of yourself. When something is special to you, take good care of it. You are special, so take care of yourself. If you don't, nobody else will.

Let love for others be constant in your heart. Ask God to occupy your heart and help you to give unconditional love to others.

Forgive those who have done you wrong. Don't give them a chance to control your heart, mind, and soul through ruthlessness. Let the peace of God reign in your heart.

Don't take on the pressures of tomorrow. Work through today with today's problems. Live life one day at a time. Things always work out.

Don't become too attached to anything in this world so that you block the flow of your blessing. What you have is for you to use temporarily while you are here.

Life is a teacher. Learn all the lessons you can and move on to being a better student. If it hands you a lemon, make lemonade. Make the choice to be a victor and not a victim. A better you, you will be for tomorrow.

Bibliography

Babcock, Maltbie, D. *Quotations by Maltbie D. Babcock*: http://strangewondrous.net/browse/author/b/babcock+maltibie+d.

Brown, Les. *Live Your Dreams.* New York: HarperCollins, 1992.

Dyer, Wayne. *The Secret of Manifesting Your Destiny*. New York: Simon & Schuster, 2002.

———. *You'll See It When You Believe It: The Way to Your Personal Transformation.* New York: Simon & Schuster, 2003.

———.*The Power of Intention.* Carlsbad, California: Hay House, 2010.

Carey, John. *How to Get What You Want and Have What You Want*. New York: HarperCollins, 1999.

Covey, Sean. *The Seven Habits of Effective Teens.* New York: Simon and Schuster, 1989.

Covey, Stephen. *The Seven Habits of Effective People.* New York: Free Press, 1989.

Cousens, Gabriel. *Conscious Eating.* Berkely, CA: Vision House International, 2000.

Grellet, Stephen. (1773-1855): http://www.values.com/inspirational-quotes13290+shall-pass-this-

Hill, Napoleon. *Think and Grow Rich.* New York: Ballante Books, 1960.

Kimbro, Dennis. *Daily Motivations for African American Success.* New York: Random House Publishing, 1993.

Leach, Reggie. *Laura Moncur's Motivational Quotations #1963*: http://www.quotationpage.com/quote/1963html

Munroe, Myles. *Understanding Your Potential.* Shippensburg, PA: Destiny Image, 1991.

Murray, W.H. *The Goethe Society of North America*: http://www.goethesociety.org/pages/quotescom.html

Seawood, Brian Luke. *Health of the Human Spirit.* Boston: Allyn and Bacon, 2001.

Schuller, Robert H. *Believe in the God Who Believes in You.* Darya Ganj, New Delhi: Orient Paperbacks, 2006.

CPSIA information can be obtained
at www.ICGtesting.com
Printed in the USA
FFOW01n1728261015
17912FF